Bedtime Stories & Guided Meditations for Busy Adults:

Beginner Meditation & Relaxing Deep Sleep Stories For Insomnia, Stress-Relief, Anxiety, Mindfulness & A Full Nights Rest

© **Copyright 2020 - All rights reserved.**

The content contained within this book may not be reproduced, duplicated or transmitted without direct written permission from the author or the publisher.

Under no circumstances will any blame or legal responsibility be held against the publisher, or author, for any damages, reparation, or monetary loss due to the information contained within this book; either directly or indirectly.

Legal Notice:

This book is copyright protected. This book is only for personal use. You cannot amend, distribute, sell, use, quote or paraphrase any part, or the content within this book, without the consent of the author or publisher.

Disclaimer Notice:

Please note the information contained within this document is for educational and entertainment purposes only. All effort has been executed to present accurate, up to date, and reliable, complete information. No warranties of any kind are declared or implied. Readers acknowledge that the author is not engaging in the rendering of legal, financial, medical or professional advice.

Table of Contents

Anxiety Guided Meditation (30mns) 1

Stress Relieving Guided Meditation (30mns) 11

Guided Meditation to Reduce Anxiety (30mns) 19

Morning Anxiety Reducing Meditation to Kick Start Your Day! (30mns) 29

Guided Mindfulness Meditation to Help Reduce Stress and Anxiety (20mns) 37

After Work Stress Relieving Meditation (30mns) 44

Before Sleep Deep Relaxation Meditation (30mns) 53

Guided Meditation for Deep Sleep (30mns) 60

Panic Attack Relaxation meditation (10mns) 66

Morning Mood Booster Meditation (10mns) 70

Lunchtime Relaxation Meditation (15mns) 74

Quick Anxiety Reducing Meditation (15mns) 78

Guided Self-Healing Meditation (30mns) 83

Easy to Follow Self-Healing Meditation (20mns) 92

Guided Sleep Meditation (20mns) 98

Stress Relief Meditation (30mns) 104

Calming After a Panic Attack Meditation (20mns) 114

Deep Relaxation Meditation (20mns) 119

Adult Bedtime Story 1 (60mns) 125

Sleep Hypnosis for Deep Sleep and Relaxation (60mns) 147

Before Sleep Hypnosis for Relaxation (60mns) 158

Anxiety Guided Meditation (30mns)

Hello and welcome to this anxiety-relieving guided meditation. In today's session, we will go on a journey toward inner peace. At the end of this journey, your consciousness will return to reality and your body, mind, and soul will be replenished and rejuvenated.

Without further, go ahead and get into a comfortable position, be it laying down or sitting up. Comfort is of the utmost importance when you need to attain full relaxation.

Right now, you do not even have to close your eyes. Just take a deep breath now and relax. Tell your body and mind that now is the time to unwind and relax. There is nothing else you need to do right now but to enjoy the stillness of the present moment.

Right now, you just have to breathe. Your eyes and mind may wander, but that is quite alright. Let them wander as they please. Sometimes, the key to calming the mind is to let it run and expend all energy. After that, you can bring it under your control.

Take another deep breath and feel your mind becoming stiller and calmer. At each breath you take, you are bringing more relaxation.

Through your nose, inhale slowly and let the air fill your lungs. Hold your breath at the top for 3 seconds. Then, through your mouth, exhale slowly. Feel the air flowing through your body through the entire breathing cycle.

Excellent. Now, continue to do this for a minute.

(Pause 1mn)

Perfect. Now, as you breathe in, slowly close your eyes. With your eyes closed, feel the stillness in your body as you hold your breath for that 3 seconds. After that, open your eyes again as you exhale. Again, feel how the air flows in and out of your body. This time, you just have to open and close your eyes as you inhale and exhale. This time, you just have to notice the stillness when you hold your breath. We will work toward bringing this stillness to calm the mind and relax the body. Continue to do this for another minute.

(Pause 1mn)

Right now, your eyes should feel very heavy and you might want to close your eyes. If so, go ahead and close your eyes now. Now is the time to dive deeply into relaxation. Now is the time to work on relaxing the mind and body.

As your vision fades to black, shift your focus to your breathing. Continue to breathe just like you have been and focus intensely on the sensations you feel as you breathe. Continue to do this for another minute.

(Pause 1mn)

Excellent. You may now continue to breathe as you normally would. At this point, your mind might still wander from one thought to another. It might bring up some random memory. Some of it might be a pleasant memory back from your childhood when things were simple. Some thoughts might be disturbing. The mind may bring up embarrassing secrets about yourself. It might bring up the very thought that caused your anxiety in the first place.

We have given the mind enough time to roam as it pleased. Now, we bring it under control. Throughout this session, whenever your mind wanders, simply guide it back to your breathing.

As we go along, sinking deeper and deeper into relaxation, continue to breathe deeply. Feel the air completely filling your lungs. Breathe deeply and as you do so, feel your body soaking up all that positive energy. When you exhale, feel the negative energy being swept away by the power of your breath alone.

Now, let us work on relaxing the body. You see, whenever the mind thinks of distressing thoughts, the body becomes nervous and twitchy. You cannot function at your best like this.

Therefore, by soothing the body, one also soothes the mind that is the center of anxiety. We can achieve this through the power of breathing alone. But first, let us start with a simple body scan exercise and then use the healing power of breathing to soothe any areas that are tense or stressed.

First, bring your attention to your toes. Wiggle your toes and feel where they are tense or sore. If you notice any tension in your toes, let it melt away as you breathe.

Now bring your attention to your feet. Wiggle your feet a little bit. Tense and flex the muscles in your feet as tightly as you can and then let it go. Feel the tension in your feet melt away and allow them to relax.

What about your ankles? Shift your attention to that area now. Perhaps move your feet around a little bit to engage your ankles. Allow them to relax as much as possible. Scan your ankles for any points of tension and just let it all melt away as you breathe.

Now focus on your calf muscles on the bottom half of your legs. Squeeze your calf muscles tightly and then let go. Relax completely and let all the tension in your legs melt away.

Next focus on your knees. Is there any soreness or tension in your knees? Where are they sore? Now, tense your body as tightly as you possibly can and hold, before completely releasing and relaxing your whole body.

Clenched every muscle tightly…
And relax, letting go…
And again, tense your body as tightly as you can.
Tighten your body as if you are squeezing out all the tension from your body…

And relax, letting go now of all the tension and completely relaxing your body…

For the final time, tense your body as tightly as you can…

Squeeze every muscle as hard as you can…

And relax… letting go now of all the tension and completely, relaxing your body.

Now, go through your body again and focus on each and every area of your body. Look for any tense or stressed areas. If you ever find one, imagine that the breath you take in flows directly to that area and wash away all the stress or tension.

Your body knows what it needs to unwind and relax. You just need to continue to breathe and introduce that healing energy into your body through your nose and push away all the negative energy as you exhale.

Let your knees complete relax… Unwind and relax…

Now focus on the upper half of your legs. Without moving your legs too much, tense up your upper leg muscles and then relax them and let go. Feel the tension you keep in your legs melt away and become fully relaxed.

Now bring your attention to your pelvic area. Feel where your body is sitting or lying. Feel where your pelvis touches the seat or where it touches where you are lying. Scan for areas of tension or discomfort.

Now, imagine that the air that you breathe in has a bright yellow color to it, imagine that it has powerful healing energy and that your body is soaking up all of its positive energy to heal as you breathe.

Introduce that energy to every part of your body and feel as your muscles relax and your tension starts to drift away. Now bring your attention to your lower back. Many of us carry around tension in our lower backs. Where do you feel pain?

Visualize yourself sending healing energy to these areas and feel the tension being to melt away. Next move your attention to the font of your body, your stomach. Feel your stomach rise and fall as you breathe in and out.

Our stomachs are often where we feel things first, this is why we say things like "I have a gut feeling this is a good or bad idea. It's also why we often get indigestion or nausea when we are dealing with highly stressful events.

Allow your stomach to lengthen, to soften, to relax. Feel all the tension in your stomach melt away as you breathe. Now, continue to bring this positive energy with your breathing up to your chest, your heart, the center of your being.

Maybe you can feel or hear your heart beating. Allow yourself to fully experience this. Allow all tension in the body to fade away as you exhale. Next, bring your attention to your upper back behind your chest.

Our upper back suffers a lot from both the stress we carry and our long hours sitting at work, often typing on computers. Feel your breath enter your body and your ribs expand. Breath out all of the tension and stress in your back and completely relax.

Next, shift your focus to your shoulders, which is another common place for tension. Perhaps you sometimes feel like you are carrying the weight of the world on your shoulders alone. Perhaps you do not have to carry this burden alone. Even if you do, now is not the time to carry it. Now is the time to unwind and relax…

And so, introduce that healing aura to your shoulders and let them droop down, let them rest in their natural position. Feel all the stress and tension released, as it slowly drifts away.

What about your neck? Does it feel sore or tense? If so, where? Where are you holding onto tension? As you exhale, allow the air to wash away all that tension and stress from your neck. Feel it becoming softer and softer, no longer rigid as you normally feel.

Now, let us focus on your face. Allow your mouth, cheek, jaw, and tongue to relax, to loosen, and to return to their natural positions. Squint up your face as hard as you can and then let it all go. Relax your face muscles and let the tension melt away.

Move your focus to your eyes and forehead. Are you squeezing your eyes? Are you furrowing your brows? Is your forehead relaxed? Are you holding tension here? If so, continue to breathe intently and feel the soothing aura going to that area and relaxes it. Feel this tension melt away as you begin to fully relax.

Lastly, bring your attention to the top and back of your head. Is there any tension here? If so, allow your breath to carry away all that tension. Continue to breathe intently and allow your breathing to carry away all the tension and stress from your body.

By now you should be fully relaxed. Enjoy this feeling. When you are ready, simply take a deep breath and slowly open your eyes. This concludes our meditation. Thank you and have a nice day.

Stress Relieving Guided Meditation (30mns)

Hello and welcome to this stress relieving guided meditation. In this session, we will work toward unwinding and relaxing the mind and body after a long day of work. Without further ado, let's get started.

Start by getting into a comfortable position. You can either sit or lay down, whatever works for you. It is fine so long as you are comfortable. After all, comfort is very important for a productive meditation session.

Once you are ready, go ahead and close your eyes. Take a few deep breaths now to tell your body that it is time to relax. On your next breath in, inhale through your nose, holding your breath at the top and count to 3 before exhaling through your mouth.

Slowly breathing in... 1... 2... 3... And slowly out...

Excellent. Now continue to do this for a while.

(Pause 1mn)

At this point, your mind may start to wander. It might bring up certain thoughts, some are positive and others are negative. Whatever those thoughts are, simply acknowledge their existence and shift your focus back to your breathing. But do not beat yourself up for it because it is natural for the mind to wander from time to time.

Now, you may allow your breathing to return to its natural rhythm. Let us work on washing away the stress in your body. So as you breathe, scan through your body and notice any tension in your body.

Starting from the top of your head, slowly shift your focus down your body. Focus on the forehead now and notice whether your forehead is tense. If it is, allow your breathing to soothe that area. Feel the air flowing in to your forehead and feel it brushing gently against your forehead as if it is gently brushing away the tension in your forehead.

Repeat this process as you go down, to the brows, eyelids, nose, cheek, jaw, lips… If you are holding onto any tension in any of those areas, use the power of your breathing to brush away the tension.

Allow your jaw to slack slightly and your tongue to return to their natural position. Take another deep breath again and feel every muscle in your head relaxing just as you exhale.

Going down to the torso now... Allow your shoulders to rest and your chest to expand and contract gently as you breathe. Feel your stomach rising and falling as you continue to breathe deeply, filling your lungs with the air that your body needs to relax. Feel your back relaxing at each breath.

Send down that positive and relaxing energy to your arms and legs. Feel the muscles in that area becoming soft and relaxed. Allow your fingers to return to their natural positions.

As you breathe, scan through your body again and notice any tense muscles in your body...

Let your breathing soothes those muscles... As if the air you let out takes away the tension in your body...

You may notice that your face is tense, or you may notice certain areas of your body are tense that you did not realize before...

You can only see them once you are in deep relaxation...

So, breathe...

In...

And out...

Let's start with thoroughly relaxing your entire body, just with deep breathing. Start intentionally breathing deep and slow now...

(Pause 2mn)

Try not to hold any parts of your body in any position... Relax and let them fall into their natural resting position...

Now, picture yourself at the beach on a beautiful sunny day. The sky above is deep blue and you could see some white clouds drifting slowly. You notice one that looks like a rabbit. The other, a face. They drift across the sky in an unhurried pace as the gentle breeze blows by.

Take a deep breath now and feel this warm breeze brushing against your body and feel yourself sinking deeper into relaxation. Focus on the warmth of the sun and use that warmth to help you to begin to help you begin to relax all of the muscles of your body.

Feel every part of your body becoming enveloped by this pleasant and relaxing sensation, from the top of your head down to your toes. Your entire body is now drenched in the warmth of the sun. Feel your every nerve and muscle becoming heavy and relaxed.

Your breathing is deep, slow, and easy. You are calm. You are at peace as you drift deeper and deeper into a state of relaxation and peace.

Take another deep breath now and feel the warm breeze washing over you. Smell that saltiness in the air. You can hear seagulls in the distance. It is indeed a wonderfully warm and peaceful day.

You look down now and see the white sand below your feet.

As you wiggle your toes to feel the fine, ivory sand slinking between your toes, you notice a few small, vibrant shells close by.

Feel yourself becoming more and more relaxed as you appreciate this feeling and quiet moment You listen to the sound of the wave washing over the shore, crashing over the breach, and flow back out again.

Synchronize your breathing with the waves. As they crash in, breathe in. As they flow back out to the sea, exhale. With each wave, you can feel yourself becoming more and more relaxed… More and more comfortable… And more and more at peace…

Any discomforts you may be feeling now start to dissipate with each wave. As you look out over the surface of the ocean, the water is crystal clear and you can see the sands swirling softly beneath the water as each wave come and go.

Look over the horizon and notice sailboats in the distance as they glide along the surface of the water. You watch the cloud move and change shape above you.

Notice the seagulls gliding over the sea. Imagine yourself riding on their backs and going far beyond the vast expanse of the sea.

Now, take in a deep breath.
Breathe in…
And out…

Feel yourself becoming warmer, cozier, more relaxed, and comfortable. Feel the sun overhead and appreciate the sense of warmth that starts from the top of your head and flowing down to your toes, allowing you to relax completely.

You now lay down a blanket on the beach and lie down to sunbathe. You feel the warmth of the sun washing over your entire body. You close your eyes and settle in, feeling relaxed even more.

It is a lovely day. You just lay there and listen to the soothing sound of the crashing waves. Each wave washes away your tensions and worries, carrying them away out to the sea.

You are now fully settled into your sanctuary. You can return to this place whenever you wish to find a sense of deep relaxation and comfort.

You may notice a symbol or shape that represents this place. Think of the symbol as the key to enter this wonderful, comfortable safe haven.

Thinking of this symbol alone helps you relax. You can access this place at any time as it is available to you at all times.

Now, it is time to return to the real world once more. Whenever you are ready, count down from 5 to 1.

As you count, you become more and more alert until you become fully awake at one, while still maintaining this deep sense of peace and relaxation. Let us begin…

5… Slowly coming back now…

4…

3… Starting to coming back to reality…

2… You can now open your eyes.

1… You are fully relaxed. Thank you and have a nice day.

Guided Meditation to Reduce Anxiety (30mns)

Hello and welcome to this guided anxiety reduction meditation. In this session, we will help you give your body that much-needed break from all your anxiety, a liberation from tension, and to give you a state of physical and mental calmness by focusing on breathing, observing the state of your body, relaxing your tense muscles, and to calm your thoughts.

So let us begin. Get into a comfortable position and lay down in your bed. You may put your arms and legs however you want as long as you are comfortable. If at any point during this session, you start to feel any discomfort, you can move your body a bit to ease that discomfort.

Go ahead and inhale slowly and deeply as your eyes close. As your vision fades to black, take another deep breath and notice how the air flows in and out of your body. Take a third deep breath and signal to the body and mind that it is time to unwind and relax.

Keep this slow and steady breathing, completely filling and emptying your lungs at each breath. Your deep breathing relaxes and calms you. It allows your body to relax, to get enough oxygen, and to feel calm.

Remain in this position. There is nothing you need to do right now and nowhere you need to be. You just need to be here, relax, and enjoy this time for yourself.

Take your time and enjoy this time for yourself. Maybe you have been through a lot, you know? Your body and mind are tired and yet you might feel that you could do something much more. Maybe you are worried about a future event. Maybe you are worried that you are not good enough.

But whatever you might be thinking right now, you do not have to worry about it now. This is the time to unwind and relax. This relaxation time will help you to be calm and healthy. This session is your productive, health time. You are doing yourself a favor by taking care of your mental health with this sleep anxiety relaxation meditation.

As you maintain your deep and steady breathing, turn your attention to your body. Notice how it feels physically. Do not do anything about it. Just be aware of the sensations in your body.

At this point, you just have to observe your body and let it tell you where the tensions are. The mind and body will guide you. Whatever it is you feel right now, recognize that it is okay. You should not concern with your physical sensations. However, some pleasant ones may be because they are signs of built-up stress.

So, take a moment and notice how you are feeling. Note any signs of stress and tension you have, again, without trying to do anything about it yet.

Scan your entire body, from the top of your head and move downward slowly.

Start focusing on your head. Observe how your head feels against the pillow or whatever beneath it.

Then, start to move your attention down to your eyes, nose, chin, then your shoulders. Notice each area as you focus your attention on it. Observe how your body feels.

Keep scanning your body. Gradually focus your attention on lower and lower parts of your body. How does your upper body feel? Note any areas of tension.

As you move to the center of your body, around the level of your stomach, note how this part of your body is feeling. Keep observing your physical state. Continue to scan your body as you shift your focus lower and lower.

Keep doing this to the level of your hips. Keep observing and shifting your attention down. How do you feel at this part of your body? Notice tensions in this part without trying to change anything. Once again, move your focus downward.

At the level of your knees, again, notice how this area feels. Notice any tension in that area. Continue to look for any signs of tension until you reach your feet.

Now, take another moment to scan your entire body. Note how your body feels as a whole. We will start now and work on soothing that tension in your body.

Starting with the area that causes you the most discomfort, focus intently on that area. On your next breath in, feel that cool breeze going straight to that area, soothing the muscles there. Feel your muscles in that spot loosening up letting go of their tension. Imagine them relaxing, releasing the tension bit by bit until the area relax.

Feel that tension loosening its grip from your body. Feel the muscles loosening up slowly, bit by bit, stretching, relaxing, becoming soft as if they are melting.

Continue to do this for the rest of your body until all areas of tension are taken care of.

(Pause 2mns)

Now, on your next breath in, breathe in through your nose, holding it at the top and count to 3, and breathe out. When you hold your breath, notice how it feels. Notice the stillness in the air as you hold your breath. Study its essence as we will introduce its peacefulness to the rest of the body. Continue to breathe this way for another minute.

(Pause 1mn)

Now that you have understood the essence of that tranquil stillness, let us work on introducing this to the body so that you may be thoroughly relaxed. Imagine this sensation spreading from your mind, moving slowly to other parts of the body. Think of it as an aura that flows slowly through your body.

Feel your body becoming more and more relaxed as this stillness, this peacefulness, this magical aura spreads throughout your body. At each breath you take, feel yourself sinking deeper and deeper into relaxation.

Imagine that the air you breathe contains some healing properties, the positive energy that your body needs to relax. Imagine that the air you breathe in is relaxation and peace. As you breathe in, feel your body soaking up all this positive energy. As you breathe out, feel yourself pushing out the tension from your body, just like how the waves recede.

Feel this relaxation as you take each and every breath. Expel the tension in your body as you exhale through your mouth. Continue to take in relaxation through the nose and push out tension through your mouth. Continue doing this as you let your body relax.

Feel yourself becoming more and more relaxed as you continue to breathe.

Breathe in...

And breathe out...

Each breath you take adds to the relaxation. Each breath you push out takes away the tension.

Keep your breathing slow and steady and feel your body becoming more relaxed with each breath. Continue to do this for a minute.

(Pause 1mn)

You now feel calm, relaxed. Your body is calm and your mind is clear... Breathing in relaxation and breathing out relaxation.

Take a deep breath in... and relax...
Now, breathe out... Relax...

Keep your breathing slow and steady. Maintain your pace and feel your body relaxing more and more deeply with each breath you take. You do not need anything now. Just rest and enjoy this relaxing sensation.

(Pause 1mn)

Now, focus on your thoughts. Notice your calm thoughts as you are enjoying this relaxation. You can attain complete calm and relaxation just by focusing on a single word. Meditate now and focus on the word "relax" by mentally saying it each time you breathe in and out.

Breathe in, "relax"
Breathe out, "relax"

Continue your slow and steady breathing, saying "relax" in your mind each time you breathe in and again when you breathe out. Continue doing this for a while.

(Pause 1mn)

It is fine if your mind starts to wander since they will, as it is only natural. Do not beat yourself up for it. Simply guide your focus back to your breathing, and tell yourself to relax. Repeat the word "relax" as you continue with this meditation.

Focus... Relax...

Keep repeating this word...

Notice how you are now completely relaxed and calm, drifting into a state of relaxation and sleepiness. You can let your mind drift. Now is the time to let your mind wander. You do not need to focus on anything at all.

Just... Rest... Relax... And enjoy this pleasant state you are in. Continue to relax and enjoy this pleasant, calm sensation. Enjoy this time you have for yourself. You deserve this peacefulness.

Remember that you have now created a space for yourself. You can return to this place of peace whenever you need to take a break. Even after you leave this place, the feeling of calm will remain with you wherever you go...

This feeling of calm and confidence will be there by your side as you about your daily life, even when you encounter stress... In fact, you can access this place of peace just by thinking about it when you start to feel anxious. You may find that the anxiety goes away in an instant.,

You may even be able to keep this relaxed feeling with you even when you encounter stressful situations. Imagine the confidence and composure you will display as you face stress while still feeling calm.

Take a deep breath in...
Relaxation breathing...
And breathe out... Emptying your lungs...

Keep breathing calmly and smoothly. Maintain this breathing cycle. Taking in relaxation and pushing out the tension that accumulates throughout the day. Imagine how every breath you take helps you become resilient against the harsh reality of life. That you are now able to cope with the stresses that come your way.

As we come to the conclusion of this meditation, you can remain here for as long as you like and enjoy this beautiful beach you have created for yourself. Whenever you are ready to return to reality, simply take a deep breath and slowly open your eyes.

Thank you.

Morning Anxiety Reducing Meditation to Kick Start Your Day! (30mns)

Hello and welcome to this morning anxiety reduction meditation. In this session, we will work on focusing your senses and calming your nerves for whatever it is that awaits you in the near future. Maybe you are anxious about an upcoming interview. Maybe it is a date, perhaps. Whatever the occasion may be, you will feel calm after this session.

So go ahead now and get into a comfortable position. You can sit or lay down however you want so long as you are comfortable. The idea is to thoroughly relax your entire body. Then, close your eyes and shift your focus to your breathing.

Now, start to scan your entire body and noting any tension in your body as well as noticing where you feel a lightness or ease. Then, scan your emotional body to notice any feelings or stress as well as emotional lightness, or something you feel good about….

Then, check in with your mind. Notice if today is one of those days full of worrying thoughts. Or if today is a good day and that you feel peaceful and quiet.

Then, focus on your breathing. Notice how it flows in and out of your body. Feel the air as it fills and deflates your lungs. Notice how your chest gently rises and falls at each breath you take.

You may notice that the air does not flow as smoothly. Maybe your breaths are shallow. Maybe you feel constrained. You can start to take deeper breaths… First into the belly… In… And out…

Then from the chest… In… And out…

Then focus on your upper back as you breathe… In… And out…

Now, repeat the breathing cycle again but holding the breath, starting from the belly… In… Hold… And out…

From the chest… In… Hold… And out…

Focusing on your upper back now… In… Hold… And out…

Breathe deep and slow…

As you continue to breathe, imagine the tension in your body fading away, washed out from your body as you exhale. As you continue to breathe deeply and calmly, check in with your body again and look for any signs of tension.

Let your breathing soothes those nervous, anxious muscles. As if the air you let out takes away the tension in your body. You may notice that your face is tense, or you may notice certain areas of your body are tense that you did not realize before.

You can only see them once you are in deep relaxation…

So, breathe…

In…

And out…

Imagine the breath swirling throughout your body, and sweeping up all the tension in your body and mind before flowing out of your body once more. At each breathe you take, feel it going to every nook and cranny of your body... Your arms, legs, fingertips and toes, ribs and hips, up to the neck, head, and even ears...

At each breath you take, feel your body being nourished and the oxygen going to every place in your body...

At each breath, you take in nourishment your body needs, and let out any stress and tension in your body and mind...

Continue to breathe as you start to clear your mind from any mental chatter, allowing it to be fully focused on sensing the entire body.

Imagine you inhaling clarity, a sense of well-being, and calm, and let them manifest in your body as you hold your breath at the top, and then release stress...

At each breath you take in, you fortify, strengthen, and refresh the body. At each exhale, you let go of all that no longer serves you...

Breathe slowly and deeply...

In...

Hold...

And out...

You choose a memory of how it really feels when you achieve something because many years ago, you achieved many goals. You realized your level of talent because you overcame something big that put you on the path to where you are now and you know that it took courage.

It took perseverance. It took persistence and it took your tenacity to never give up and you never gave up. You did it.

I'm talking about learning to walk. You know at first it wasn't easy pulling yourself up and then sometimes falling down, pulling up, and falling down again. But you persevered. You found the courage from somewhere. There was no way you were giving up and then one day your legs seemed so much stronger.

So much more able to carry your weight. Your whole frame was more stable, more robust because you trusted in yourself as you have really trusted yourself before. And now today, you know you can just put one foot in front of the other without even thinking about it.

At that time there was a massive sense of achievement.

You did this against all odds and as the days and weeks and months go by, you get stronger, faster, and more confident. You never look back and you chose not to look back when you decided to move forward.

When you think in this way and when you feel in this way, you really do know that anything is possible. Anything is possible for you as you contemplate what is ahead.

You can imagine your mind is successful in its stillness and calmness. Just silently enjoying and witnessing these moments of success, fascinated and excited by those abilities that you have deep inside to learn and do whatever it is you need to learn and do.

Your mind knows exactly how to learn and achieve and succeed. It is still with you today. That part of you is still with you right now.

All of those talents that have been hiding within you can now be released and expressed as you become your most authentic, successful, invigorated, and inspired self.

But you can learn new ways of thinking, new ways of responding, new ways of feeling, new ways of acting because the patterns of living that we all do are just patterns.

They really are just a habit that you choose because your mind is so much more powerful and perhaps you even know your mind is so much more powerful than you know.

And just like learning to walk, you can overcome any challenge.

You can overcome any challenge, any barrier, any limiting belief. You can overcome and move past any barrier, any limiting belief as you make the decision now to just let go of those old ways that had previously held you back.

Let go of the old way, soaking up that which is valuable, taking one step at a time.

Slowly, easily, naturally, you are successful. You are inspired. You are motivated.

You know you can do, what you set out to achieve, and now in your own time, allow yourself to become more aware.

Moving up towards the surface now, coming back to the present, and now slowly in your own time.

Allow yourself to become more aware or aware of your conscious surroundings. Perhaps gently moving your fingers and your toes.

Becoming aware of your physical sensations and your physical body and when you are ready, gently allow your eyes to open. Moving up now towards the surface of your conscious awareness, coming back fully to the present, feeling refreshed, energized, and motivated to start your new day.

Feeling, refreshed, energized, inspired, and motivated completely to start your very new day. You are now ready to tackle everything in your path. You are unstoppable.

Take your time to enjoy this unhurried moment. Allow yourself to immerse in the meditation and give your body and mind full attention…

Notice any tense areas in your body or mind and breathe away to relax them…

As you come to the end of this meditation session, take another deep breath and smile as you have given yourself time and attention. Slowly open your eyes when you are ready to start your day. Have a great day and I wish you all the very best.

Guided Mindfulness Meditation to Help Reduce Stress and Anxiety (20mns)

Hello and welcome to this guided mindfulness meditation to reduce stress and anxiety. In this session, we will work on relaxing the body and mind, thus liberating them from the grips of stress and anxiety.

To begin, get into a comfortable position. You can either lay down or sit. If at any point during this session, you start to feel any discomfort in any area of your body, you may shift your body a bit to ease that pain.

Without further ago, go ahead and close your eyes now and take a deep breath to tell it that it is time to unwind and relax. Then, let your mind become quiet. Turn your attention inward as you focus on relaxing your body. Let your muscles relax. From the top of your head all the way to the tips of your toes.

Now, think of what relaxation feels like. To you, it might be warm, tingly, maybe heavy yet comfortable, or light and liberating. Whatever it is, relaxation is indeed a calm, pleasant feeling. It is very comfortable.

Allow your muscles to relax and try and find any areas of your body that are tense. We shall start by relaxing the body from there. As your chest rose and fall gently as you breathe, picture yourself breathing in the relaxation in the air every time. As you breathe out, feel the tension and stress leaving your body.

As you breathe out, imagine all the tension leaves your body, riding on the air you let out of your chest. And you become even more relaxed as you breathe in the cool air. Becoming so deeply relaxed. Notice how relaxed you are.

As you breathe, any remaining tension continues to leave your body... And you become more and more relaxed.

Now is the time to relax. You just need to relax. You do not need to do anything else right now but to unwind and relax. Let go of all your worldly worries. Right now, just loosen up and relax.

Now, let's use visualization to focus your mind. Give it a mental break from all the worldly worries. Whenever worrying thoughts intrude your peace of mind, as they will, recall this serene feeling you have in your body at this very moment.

Whenever your peace of mind is intruded by worldly worries, tell yourself to breathe. The rise and fall of your chest will soothe you. Let yourself relax. Then, imagine that worry is a deep and dark place...

And peace you crave for is the light...

Stress and anxiety demand that you stay awake and shaky because of them. It is an evil power and you feel its influence when your muscles start to tense up, even when you are sleeping. It causes sore and ruins your mood, your peace of mind. This is what they do to the mind and body. They make you feel restless and tired.

Think of your peace of mind as light and sleepy element. Think of it as a loving mother, calling to you to come to her embrace. She will tell you to come to her and that she will bring you to a warm and cozy place. She will give you a nice, warm, and soft bed for you to lie on. She will tell you all the things you need to hear for your exhausted mine. She will make you feel safe, at ease. She will take you to a place of tranquility.

Now, using the power of your imagination, think of a place where you would feel peaceful. You do not have to try hard here as your subconscious mind will often take the lead and conjure up such a place.

It could be a place beyond your wildest dreams, a magnificent waterfall, a vast field of vibrant flowers, a mountaintop that pierces the clouds, a golden beach, or a thick and peaceful forest. It could be a place you have been to. Use the power of your imagination to access that place of peace.

You are there now, in the place of peace, where nothing in the world can harm you. This is the place of your own creation. You have been here a few times in the past when you are asleep. Your mind often comes here when you are unconscious.

It comes here to relax and rejuvenate. But it cannot come here often as this place is often locked. To access this place, you need to relax the mind and body. Once you do, the door opens for you. Now that you are here, you can take this place with you to the outside world, along with its powerful yet relaxing aura.

Whenever you feel stressed or anxious, you just have to close your eyes and breathe deeply. You will be transported back to this place and you will feel at ease once more. By then, nothing can harm you.

Now, take a moment to explore this place of your own making. Feel this place with all your senses. Absorb the essence of this place and feel yourself sinking deeper and deeper into relaxation.

Now, repeat this mantra after me.

"Right now, I am at peace. I am surrounded by peace. I am not in danger. Nothing can harm me."

"I am at peace. I can picture happy images with my imagination. I can recall peaceful words I have read or heard today to calm me down. I can listen to new peaceful, sleepy words that can lead me to dreamy, wonderful places."

Let relaxation happen naturally. Let the unconscious part of your brain take over. Let the soft and gentle words carry you further into relaxation. Let the words work their magic. Imagine the words you whisper to yourself coming to life and take you to that peaceful place.

Know those worrying thoughts tell your brain to stay awake as they cause tight sensations in your body and thoughts that repeat again and again in your mind. Imagine them being swept away by your breath as you breathe out, and whatever is left is erased by the kind words you whisper to yourself.

With your worries gone, go ahead now and allow yourself to drift toward peacefulness as you continue to repeat affirmations to become more and more sleepy.

"I cannot relax if I force myself to relax. Instead, I let relaxing words guide me. They can cause my mind and body to relax and deliver me to my peaceful place. My body knows how to breathe. It can do this naturally."

"I can relax and let the kind words bring me back to that peaceful place. I can attain mental tranquility. Rest and relaxation help my body rejuvenate."

Now, as we come to the conclusion of this meditation, I will count down from 10. As I do, feel yourself return to reality.

10… Slowly coming back now…

9…

8…

7… Feel the room around you…

6…

5… Take a deep breath now…

4…

3… Feel your senses returning to your body…

2…

1… And you have returned. You are fully relaxed and energized.

After Work Stress Relieving Meditation (30mns)

Hello and welcome to this after work stress relieving meditation. In this session, we will be working on cleansing both the mind and body from the stress and tension you have accumulated throughout the day.

To begin, make yourself comfortable. You can sit down or lay down, and place your arms however you like so long as you are comfortable. Comfort is important for a productive meditation session.

Go ahead and close your eyes now and focus on your own breathing. Now, take a deep breath to signal to the body that it is time to unwind and relax. Give your body and mind the permission to relax.

Tell yourself that it is important that you relax as much as possible before you sleep tonight. It is important that you get a full, restful sleep so you have the energy to tackle tomorrow's tasks, after all.

You can continue to relax as you listen and breathe. Each time you exhale, you can feel yourself becoming more and more relaxed. More and more relaxed…

Soon, you will experience relaxation and you are probably wondering what that experience will be like.

Rest assured that no matter how deeply relaxed you become, you will remain in complete control. You will stay in control even when you are very deeply immersed in the experience of relaxation.

Now, as you continue to breathe deeply and slowly, you can start to feel yourself becoming more and more relaxed... Eventually, you might even fall asleep, but that is quite alright.

Perhaps you have been working too hard lately so that your body and mind just want to go to sleep. If at any point during this meditation, you want to go to sleep, you may go to bed straight away. After all, the goal of this meditation is to get you to relax, and if you do feel sleepy, then this session is complete.

At the same time, if you feel any discomfort during this session, you may move your body gently to ease that discomfort. Do not let discomfort get in the way of your experience of relaxation.

For a moment, be aware of the normal sounds around you now and whatever you hear from now on will only help to relax you more.

As you exhale, release any tension, any stress from any part of your body your mind, your thoughts just let that stress go.

Just let any stressful thoughts rushing through your mind, feel then begin to wind down…

Wind…

Down…

Wind down and relax…

Begin with letting all the muscles in your face relax, Especially your jaw. Let your teeth part, just a little bit and relax this area. Your jaw and mouth in general are the part where your body is tensest. Most tension and stress gather here.

As such, spend extra time in this area and relax your jaw. Feel that relaxation coming in, going to your temples and relaxing the muscles in your temples. As you think about relaxing, those muscles will just relax. Feel them relax. As you relax, you'll be able to just drift off and float into a deeper and deeper level of total relaxation.

You will continue to relax.

Now, let all of the muscles in your forehead. Relax. Feel those muscles smooth, smooth, and relaxed.

Rest your eyes.

Just imagine that your eyelids are feeling so comfortable, so pleasant, so heavy and so relaxed.

Now, let all the muscles on the back of your neck and shoulders relax as well.

Feel a heavy, heavy weight being lifted off your shoulders and you feel relieved, lighter, and more relaxed.

All of the muscles in the back of your neck and shoulders relax and feel that soothing relaxation.

Go down your back, down, and down, and down to the lower part of your back.

Those muscles just let go with every breath you take and exhale, you're just feeling your body drifting and floating.

Deeper and deeper down…

Deeper down into total relaxation and all that is here now.

Let your muscles go relaxing more and more. Let all of the muscles in your shoulders running down your arms, to your fingertips.

Relax, and let your arms feel so heavy…

So heavy…

So heavy, so comfortable…

So pleasant…

and relaxed...

You may have tingling in your fingertips. That's perfectly fine. You may have warmth in the palms of your hands.

They are so relaxed. they are so heavy, so heavy and so relaxed.

Now, you inhale once again, and relax those chest muscles, and now as you exhale feel your stomach muscles relax.

As you exhale, relax all of the muscles in your stomach. Let them go.

All of the muscles your legs, feel them relax. All of the muscles your legs, so completely relaxed right to the tips of your toes.

You are noticing how very comfortable your body feels.

Just drifting and floating...

Deeper...

Deeper...

Relaxed...

Now, imagine a spreading sense of calm and peace spreading throughout your body. Let go of all of your cares and concerns. Let them drift away like clouds in the wind, dissipating more and more.

Take another deep breath and relax… Let go of your entire body and allow it to be supported by whatever it is that is beneath you. Feel your body loosening up. Shift your focus to the top of your head now and continue to breathe deeply, letting the rejuvenating properties in the air to heal, to loosen, and to relax those areas.

Introduce that healing energy to every single part of your body. Starting from the top of your head, and work your way slowly down toward the tip of your toes. Feel each and every part of your body loosening up and going limb. Feel every single muscle in your body relaxing as you breathe.

Now that your body is entirely at ease, you can start to imagine being somewhere peaceful and relaxing. Perhaps you can picture yourself sunbathing on a quiet beach on a warm sunny day with a beautiful blue sky. But you can imagine being anywhere you like, even in fictional locations. So long as you can feel relaxed and at ease, it is perfect.

That place should be a safe haven for you, somewhere you want to be, or where you can be yourself. You can imagine yourself being there with your mind's eye, and since all the things your body would sense.

This is a safe haven for you, created by the subconscious mind. The magical thing about this place is that it has always been there, in your dreams, but you did not know how to access this place yet. Normally, you can only find this place when you are totally at peace, which usually happens while you are asleep.

Now that you are at total peace, you can access this place again. This time, you can bring it with you to the outside world. That way, when you find yourself stressed or tense, you can simply return to this place through meditation.

Now that you are in your perfect world, take some time to enjoy this place. Sense it with all your senses and take in all its essence so that you may heal and relax even further.

(Pause 1mn)

Inhale deeply and start to close your eyes gently. Relax. And as you are relaxing deeper and deeper, imagine a beautiful staircase leading you to a very peaceful, a very special place for you.

You can imagine it to be any place you choose. Perhaps you would enjoy a beach, or ocean with clean fresh air, or the mountain with a stream and a river. Any place is perfectly fine.

At each breath, you take, imagine you take each step down the staircase and relax even deeper...

(Pause 1mn)

Imagine a peaceful and special place, a place of peacefulness, and soft love. You can imagine this special place and perhaps you can also feel it. Feel the atmosphere here now.

You are here and there is no one to disturb you. Allow yourself to be here now, feeling that sense of peace through you, behind you within you, before you and after you.

Allow this sense of your own special atmosphere of peace and love, this sense of well-being, to stay with you in this space within you, open and alive, long after this session is completed for the rest of this day and evening and tomorrow.

Allow yourself to allow this peace and love to be stronger to come to life, feeling at peace with the sense of wellbeing. Each and every time that you choose to do this kind of relaxation you'll be able to relax deeply and deeper, regardless of the stress and tension that may surround your life.

You are now very deeply relaxed, completely at one with yourself, completely engrossed. Now, focus solely on your special place. Just be there now and know that you are at peace. Calm and relaxed.

There is no tension, no anxiety. Concentrate on this feeling and know that you can take it with you throughout your day tomorrow. No stress or anxiety shall intrude on your mental tranquility. Whenever you are stressed, you can turn to your special place and breathe to allow your body to be calm once more.

Finally, take another deep breath and smile. We are coming to the conclusion of this meditation. Whenever you are ready to go back to reality, simply take another deep breath and open your eyes. For now, you can remain here for as long as you like.

Before Sleep Deep Relaxation Meditation (30mns)

Hello and welcome to this pre-sleep deep relaxation meditation. This meditation is designed to help you relax so you can get a deep, restful sleep. You will wake up the next day feeling energized and fresh.

So to begin, lie down on your bed, find a comfortable resting position, and close your eyes. Find a comfortable position with a spine straight and completely on the mattress. Let's start to check in with yourself here by scanning the physical body, noticing where you're holding tension, noticing where you might feel a lightness or ease.

Scan the emotional body checking in with any feelings of stress that you might be carrying or maybe some emotional lightness or something you're feeling good about.

(Pause 1mn)

Start to check in with your breath noticing where in your body it flows maybe you feel it in the chest.

Maybe the belly will notice where it doesn't flow. Maybe the breath is a little shallow.

(Pause 1mn)

Start to deepen the breath, drawing it first into the belly, then the chest, and upper back, and exhaling to release. Another breath into the belly, then the chest, and exhale. Start to slow the breath, holding at the top, and exhale again.

Breathe in… 1, 2, 3.
Pause at the top…
And smooth, even exhale…

Breathing at your own pace. Calm, slow, and smooth. Inhale all the way into the belly, then the chest. Pause for a moment and exhale completely, returning your focus to the physical body. It will start to release some tension, consciously releasing muscles of the face.

As you relax, see if there might have been muscles you didn't even realize you were holding. Relax the throat in the neck, feeling the back of the head sink into the ground fully supported. Relax the shoulders, letting them sink into the ground, relaxing the collarbones, the chest.

Just letting go of the weight that you're carrying. Relax the upper arms, the elbows, the forearms. Relax the hands, letting the fingers come to rest and their natural curl. Still with the breath, smooth inhales. Pausing at the top…

Then exhale, completely releasing the chest, releasing tension across the ribs, letting the middle back and the low back settles onto the ground. Relax the abdomen, relax the hips, and the buttocks, letting them release into the ground.

Relaxing the thighs, the knees, relaxing your calves, and your ankles, staying with the breath as you inhale slowly and smoothly. Pause at the top. Then exhale completely. Relax the feet, relaxing even the toes, letting them fall out to the sides. Slow, smooth inhales.

Check back in with the physical body, noticing if there are still areas where you're keeping the muscle tense, seeing if you can let go a little more, see if you can let go a little more with every exhale, not worrying about where we need to be next or what we might need to do.

Allow yourself this time to intentionally relax.

Take note of any emotional stress just as we do with the physical ones. Exhale them away. smooth long inhales. Pausing at the top. And sending any unwanted stress out with our exhales.

Again, inhale slowly and smoothly… Holding at the top… And exhale…

Allow the mind to rest on the sensation of each breath in and out through the nose.

Check back in with the physical body, noticing where you might be storing tension.

Again, releasing the jaw, releasing the muscles of the face, relaxing shoulders, relaxing the abdomen, the hips, and the legs… Letting the body feel completely supported by the ground beneath you…

Tune into the breath… Notice where in the body the air flows… Notice where it doesn't really reach…

Breathe… The belly, then the chest, and upper back… Then exhale completely… Breathe still with a slow smooth exhale, a pause the top… And release.

Inhale into the belly, then the chest, and then imagine this breath swirling all the way out through the arms and the legs... Inhale, the breath reaching all the way through the body to the fingertips and the toes.

Send this exhale swirling through the ribs and the hips up to your shoulders, imagining this breath coming up the neck into the head even the ears nourished by this inhale, sending fresh oxygen to every place in the body, sending nutrients to yourself intentionally...

Your breath swirls around the entire body, not only does it distribute what you need, it gathers up everything you no longer wish to carry.

Exhale physical tension...

Inhale a new breath... And exhale, releasing emotional stress...

Pause at the bottom before you inhale fresh air sending it all the way out through the body, arms, legs, fingers, toes, hips, shoulders, even your ears, and your nose. Exhale... Releasing any mental chatter, allowing the mind to be fully occupied by sensing as much of the body as you can at one time...

Inhale to nourish… Exhale to release sending out carbon dioxide, sending out physical tension, sending out emotional stress, sending out your mental chatter…

Inhaling clarity a sense of well-being and calm…
Pause at the top before exhaling completely…
Checking in with your breath… Filling first the belly, then the chest, and upper back, before you send this fresh air through the entire body…

Exhale… Checking in with your physical tension, noticing if you holding any tension in the legs or shoulders… and exhaling that tension away. Inhale to fortify, strengthen, and refresh the body… Exhale to let go of all that no longer serves you…

Inhale, filling the belly, then the chest before you send that fresh air to circulate in the entire body… Pause the top and exhale completely, releasing physical tension emotional stress mental chatter on the way out…

Continue these smooth full inhales at an unhurried pace…
Pause at the top and with every exhale, continue to let go…

Staying here on your back, breathing deeply for as long as you'd like and when you're ready to release yourself from this meditation, simply stretch and open your eyes if you wish. Enjoy several unhurried breaths here and smile as you have given yourself the time to relax…

This concludes the deep sleep meditation. Thank you and goodnight.

Guided Meditation for Deep Sleep (30mns)

Hello and welcome to this guided meditation for deep sleep. Here, we will be working on relaxing the mind and body so that you would get a peaceful and restful sleep. That way, you will wake up the next day, feeling totally relaxed, alert, and energized.

So, get comfortable in whatever way you see fit. It is a good idea to lay down or sit right on your bed as you can bring this meditation session to a close by going straight to bed.

Now that you are comfortably settled, go ahead, and close your eyes. If it's more comfortable for you to leave your eyes open, pick a spot that you can stare at without moving your head and focus on that.

Now, take a deep breath, letting your arms hang gently in your shoulder sockets, feeling the tips of your fingers wherever they are. If they're touching your leg, or if they're touching a chair or the floor, notice your arms and fingers hanging gently from your shoulder socket.

Take a slow, gentle breath and feel the air as it passes down your throat. Feel the sides of your chest as they gently expand and with a soft exhale.

On your next breath in, imagine yourself standing at the beach. It is a warm, sunny day and the sky is clear. It is not too hot or cold. The sand feels very fine beneath and you could hear the seagulls in the distance. On the far distance of the beach is a pier. At the end of the pier is a little sailboat and it beckons at you to come closer.

At each breath you take, feel yourself walking slowly toward this boat. As you walk, feel the fine sand beneath your feet. Feel the warm and gentle breeze brushing up against you as you walk. Hear the gentle waves as they come and go. At each breath you take, feel yourself sinking deeper into relaxation.

(Pause 1mn)

You walk up on the pier now and climb into the boat. It looks very cozy and it has a nice little hammock that is just the right size for you. The boat is full of your favorite snacks and drinks. You help yourself to these snacks and drinks as you lie on the hammock, gazing lazily at the sky above.

Taking a deep breath now, you feel the gentle wobble of the boat as it leaves the pier. You feel very safe in this boat and you know that the wind and tide will carry you to where you want to be.

Now, take another deep breath, noticing your jaw muscles as you gently let your breath out so you are standing in the boat you sit down comfortably and as you make yourself comfortable in this little boat.

You notice that the waves are gently rocking you back and forth. You are surrounded by a sense of serenity and calm. Taking a slow deep breath, you feel connected and held in all parts of your life.

At this point, your mind may start to wander and bring up random thoughts that may gladden or upset you. Whatever it is, acknowledge that the thoughts are there and let them go. Simply take a deep breath and return your focus to your place of peace, on the boat.

Continue to enjoy your time on the boat as it sails slowly across the ocean. Here, nothing can harm you. You feel at peace. You feel at ease. You feel very and thoroughly relaxed.

Eventually, you feel that the boat has come to a stop. You stand up and feel that you are exactly where you want to be. It is a place of your wildest dreams. So, take a moment now and imagine this place. Use the power of your imagination, but do not try too hard. The subconscious mind will take over and conjure up such a place that you know is a place of bountiful resources.

(Pause 1mn)

This is a magical spot just for you and you alone. This is the place where you will get everything that your mind and body need to relax and rejuvenate. So, taking a deep breath now, you may start to explore this place. Take your time and use all your senses to sense this place and absorb its magical and relaxing power.

(Pause 1mn)

Inhaling to the top of the belly the middle of the belly you receive all of the trust that you need. Completing your inhale, you receive all of the safety and security that you need. With your exhale, any fear, anger, stress, or discomfort you feel is completely released into the ocean.

In doing so, you receive all of the hope, joy, and peace you need. As you exhale all sadness, loneliness, and grief, fully and gently leave your field. Inhaling into the bottom of your belly, the middle of your belly, and on the top of your belly.

You receive all of the energy that you need, your exhale releases any fatigue, tension, or exhaustion you might be feeling. Take one more breath to receive what you need. If you want to stay here in this place for a few more breaths, feel free to do so.

(Pause 1mn)

Any tension in pain you had noticed before is gone. In fact, you were quite excited and happy that your shoulders are relaxed that your back feels loose straight and strong. You notice that your hips feel open and supported, and all tension in your legs and feet have been released.

You can return to this place of peace and tranquility at any point in the future if you like. All you have to do is to meditate and the door to this place will open for you. You can remain here for as long as you like and feel completely at ease.

Right here, right now, you feel completely safe and relaxed. Nothing can harm you. Everything you need is right here. Nothing in the outside world can harm you. No worldly worries can ruin your peace of mind. So long as you are here, you are safe.

As we come to the end of this meditation, take another deep breath and smile. Smile because you have given yourself the time and space you need to recover and relax. You can remain in this place for as long as you want and you can drift right off to sleep after this session. Thank you and goodnight.

Panic Attack Relaxation meditation (10mns)

Hello and welcome to this guided meditation for relaxation after a panic attack. In this session, we will work toward relaxing the body and mind after a stressful situation.

So, let us begin by getting into a comfortable position. You can lie down or sit and place your arms and legs however you like so long as you are comfortable. If you haven't done so already, go ahead and close your eyes. As your vision fades to black, shift your focus to your breathing.

Relax…

Take a deep breath in and slowly release it.

Continue these deep breaths, making sure to fill your lungs completely and breathe deep into your belly.

As you breathe in, feel the positive energy flowing into your body.

As you breathe out, visualize the negative energy, stress, and worries flowing out of you.

Continue to breathe this way for a few more minutes to allow the body and mind to slow down, unwind, and relax...

(Pause 3mns)

At this point, your mind may start to wander. It might bring up worrying thoughts, some of which may be caused by the panic attack you just experienced. If that is the case, simply push those thoughts aside and focus on your breathing. Use it as an anchor to hold your focus in the present moment.

Right now, there is nothing else you need to do but to unwind and relax. Unwind... And relax...

Take another deep breath to help the body relax. If your mind wanders, gently guide your focus back to your breathing.

And as you are relaxing deeper and deeper, imagine a beautiful staircase leading you to a very peaceful, a very special place for you.

You can imagine it to be any place you choose. Perhaps you would enjoy a beach, or ocean with clean fresh air, or the mountain with a stream and a river. Any place is perfectly fine.

At each breath, you take, imagine you take each step down the staircase and relax even deeper…

(Pause 1mn)

Imagine a peaceful and special place, a place of peacefulness, and soft love. You can imagine this special place and perhaps you can also feel it. Feel the atmosphere here now.

You are here and there is no one to disturb you. Allow yourself to be here now, feeling that sense of peace through you, behind you within you, before you and after you.

Allow this sense of your own special atmosphere of peace and love, this sense of well-being, to stay with you in this space within you, open and alive, long after this session is completed for the rest of this day and evening and tomorrow.

Allow yourself to allow this peace and love to be stronger to come to life, feeling at peace with the sense of wellbeing.

Each and every time that you choose to do this kind of relaxation you'll be able to relax deeply and deeper, regardless of the stress and tension that may surround your life.

You may now also remain in this peace calmer, more relaxed, allowing the tensions and stresses to bounce off and away from you…

Just bouncing off

And away from you…

And allowing this deeper sense of who you are to stay with you, growing stronger and stronger throughout the day.

As we come to the conclusion of this meditation, you can spend as much time in this place. And whenever you decide to leave, know that you can bring this place and its calming aura with you to the outside world. Whenever you feel stressed again, simply meditate once more and imagine this place.

It will take you back here and you can be free from the worldly worries again until you are ready to return. Again, remain here for as long as you like. When you are ready, simply take a deep breath and slowly open your eyes.

Thank you.

Morning Mood Booster Meditation (10mns)

Hello and welcome to this morning mood booster meditation. You've just woken up and felt ready for the day ahead, but your body and mind may not be ready. Meditation as a means to transition between a relaxed state to an alert state is recommended to start off your day right.

In this session, we will work toward calming the mind and body and bringing in more energy to them. Through the power of breathing alone, we will work toward bringing the springs back into your steps At the end of this session, you will feel refreshed and alert.

So without further ado, let's get started.

Begin by getting into a comfortable position, be it laying down or sitting up in a brightly lit and open area. Perhaps on the couch in your living room or the front or back yard. Just make sure that the place is quiet because we do not want to overwhelm the mind with stimulants too soon.

Once you are nicely settled in, take a deep breath to tell your body that it is time to wake up and prepare for the day ahead, which may be full of chaos and stress. But you need not worry about that right now.

Take another deep breath in through your nose, and let it flow out through your mouth…

In… And out…
In… And out…
In… And out…

Excellent. If your eyes are still open, go ahead and close them now. As your vision fades to black, shift your focus to your own breathing. Continue to breathe like this for another minute.

(Pause 1mn)

At this point, your mind may start to wander. It might bring up random thoughts that make you feel a certain way. Right now is the time to bring in energy to the mind and body. So, if your mind does wander, simply disregard them and focus back on your breathing.

The body and mind are very resilient. Only through imaginable and harsh circumstances can one hope to break them. So long as you are taking the time to care for your body and mind, nothing can break them and you will come back home at the end of the day, still feeling like you have some energy left to spend with your loved one and pursue your passion.

Perhaps you care for your pets or ride very carefully. For your pets, you might make sure that they are well fed and have enough toys and water while you are out at work. If you own a car, you might make sure that it has enough gas, and the engine is well taken care of. You might take care of your possessions carefully.

Now, you choose to take care of yourself. You chose to take care of yourself as if your body is your most valuable possession, which is true. Your body and mind are your most valuable possessions and you now choose to treat them with the value they deserve. This is a very precious gift to give yourself.

Take another deep breath now and smile because you have decided to give yourself a very beautiful gift. In doing so, you choose to acknowledge how valuable you really are. Maybe you have treated yourself too harshly. Maybe you did not treat yourself in a kind and gentle way.

So now take the time to give yourself love and relaxation. The day ahead might be full of chaos. It might be full of stress. But in knowing that you are well taken care of, you are alright.

So as we come to the conclusion of this meditation, you can take some time and enjoy this stillness, this calm, this tranquility. Whenever you are ready to move on, simply take a deep breath, open your eyes, and you may go on with your day.

Thank you and have a good day.

Lunchtime Relaxation Meditation (15mns)

Hello and welcome to this lunchtime relaxation meditation. It is currently midday and you still have many hours to go before your day ends. But the fact that you are here means that either your body and mind are tired already or that you simply want to take some time off to rejuvenate even though you can still get through the day just fine.

Regardless, we will work toward relaxing the body and mind and bring energy back to them so that you can continue to maintain your peak performance. So go ahead now and get into a comfortable position and get ready to meditate. Make sure that you are in a distraction-free area so you can meditate in peace.

It does not matter how you sit or lay down. Place your arms and legs however you like so long as you are comfortable. Comfort is of utmost importance for a productive meditation session, after all.

Once you are ready, take a deep breath and close your eyes. When your vision fades to black, shift your focus to your own breathing. We will be using this breathing to bring in the energy that your body needs.

So go ahead and take a deep breath now and enjoy the relaxation and energy it brings.

On your next breath in, I want you to take a deep breath through your nose and hold it at the top for 3 seconds before exhaling through your mouth. As you hold your breath, focus on the stillness.

So go ahead and take a deep breath in through your nose…

Hold it for a few seconds… Focusing on the stillness…

And exhale slowly…

As you continue to breathe this way, feel how the air flows in and out of your body. Feel the stillness in your body when you hold your breath. Continue to breathe this way for a minute.

(Pause 1mn)

At this point, your mind may start to wander. After working for some time, the mind may not have calmed down yet and it will continue to bring up random thoughts. Some of them might be about the work you will soon return to. Some of them might be about other worries that you have for the future.

Whatever those thoughts are, set them aside for now. There is plenty of time to worry but now is not that time. Simply acknowledge that you might be worried about somethings but then push those thoughts away and shift your focus back to your breathing.

Right now, you may allow your breath to return to its natural rhythm. As you continue to breathe, imagine that the air you bring into your body having that bright glow. It is the healing energy that the air carries. By breathing in deeply of that air, you are bringing that healing energy into your body.

Your body will take that energy and heal itself. It will take that energy and use it to power itself so that it may continue to function at its best throughout the day. At the same time, as you breathe out, you are using the air to dispel any negativity or stress or tension from your body.

Continue to breathe and allow your body to absorb this positive energy for a while.

(Pause 2mns)

As we come to the end of this meditation, you may continue to remain in your meditative position. Whenever you are ready to return to work again, take a deep breath and smile. Thank yourself for allowing you to take a moment to relax and rejuvenate. Thank you for allowing you to enjoy this positive. Give yourself a pat on the back and open your eyes.

Thank you and have a nice day.

Quick Anxiety Reducing Meditation (15mns)

Hello and welcome to this quick anxiety-reducing meditation. In this session, you will embark on a journey to relaxation, away from the worries of the outside world. In this place, your peaceful place, you will experience a wonderful calmness and meditative state of mind.

To begin, get into a comfortable position be it sitting or lying down. You may place your arms and legs however you want so long as you are comfortable. Comfort is of utmost importance after all and it is crucial for your relaxation.

So, go ahead now and take a deep breath, telling your body and mind that it is time to unwind and relax. This time is for you and you alone. There is nothing else you need to do at this point.

If you haven't done so already, go ahead and close your eyes now. As your vision fades to black, shift your focus to your breathing. We will use the power of breathing to calm both the mind and body down.

On your next breath, allow the air to flow in through your nose, but hold your breath for a few seconds before your exhale. Focus on the gentle stillness between your inhale and exhale. Continue to breathe this way for a while and study the essence of this gentle stillness in the air.

(Pause 1mn)

Now, let us work on relaxing the body. To do so, simply shift your focus to the top of your head and slowly move it down to the rest of your body. Starting with the forehead now, focus on that area, and introduce that stillness to your forehead. Allow the muscles to return to their natural position. Feel them soften and relax.

Going down slowly to your brows now... Take that stillness and let your brows absorb that relaxation from your breathing... Introduce that relaxation to your eyelids, nose, cheeks, lips, tongue, and jaw...

Feel tour entire head relaxing and become light as all worries are washed away, yet heavy with the aura of relaxation... Bring that peace and relaxation to your torso now, and feel it loosening up and relaxing just as I say the word "Relax"...

So... Relax... Unwind and relax... Deeper and deeper now...

Bring that relaxing aura to your limbs... Arms and legs... Let all muscles return tot heir natural position, where they can unwind and relax... Take another deep breath now and feel your fingers and toes returning to their natural positions, light and free from worries, yet heavy from relaxation...

Feel your body becoming loose and limp, free from stress, and full of relaxation... Take another deep breath to tell the body and mind to relax, to rejuvenate, to release all that tension...

You are completely in control of this meditation session, so you can return to your awakened state whenever you wish. You can do so by just opening your eyes once more.

Now, breathe in deeply and exhale fully.

Breathe in deeply...

And exhale fully...

Allow the sound of your breathing to soothe and calm your mind and soul.

Breathe in deeply...

And exhale fully...

At this point, your mind may start to wander. It might bring up some random thoughts, some are happy, some are worrying, some are sad, some that caused you so much anxiety.

This is fine. This is completely normal. Simply acknowledge that such thoughts exist and tell yourself that you will address all of those problems after this session. Just by doing this, those thoughts will begin to quiet down as you concentrate on listening to your own breathing.

As you listen to your inhale, you will find your mind gently begin to quiet down.

So, breathe in deeply, taking in the cool and refreshing air

And exhale fully, pushing out hot and tense air.

You may feel your body starting to loosen up and relaxing as you allow the sound of your own breathing to soothe your soul, taking in the infinite source of energy within you.

Just through breathing alone, you allow yourself to be in total peace with your surroundings.

Allow the sound of your breathing to continue relaxing your whole body, and take your time to enjoy this wonderful experience. You can remain in this deeply relaxed state for a while and smile as you now have completed this meditation session. You can now have a restful sleep.

Guided Self-Healing Meditation (30mns)

Hello and welcome to this guided self-healing meditation. In this session, we will work on soothing the pain and tension in your body. At the end of this session, you will feel very liberated, free from all that stress and negative energy.

So without further ado, let us get started. Simply get into a comfortable position. You can sit or lie down, whatever works for you as long as you are comfortable. It is important that you can relax so you can effectively heal your body.

If you haven't already, go ahead and close your eyes. As your vision fades to black, shift your focus to your breathing. Take a deep breath now to tell the body that it is time to unwind and relax.

Right now, there is nothing else you need to do but to relax and enjoy the relaxation. Right now is the time to relax, rejuvenate, and regain your strength. If at any moment during this meditation, you feel that any part of your body is becoming uncomfortable, you may shift slightly to ease that discomfort.

Now, let us work on soothing the body, encouraging healing energy to move to the places within the body where it is most required. Those places can focus more deeply on repairing and healing themselves, feeling stronger and healthier.

Now, take another deep breath and feel your upper torso expanding and contracting gently as you breathe. In through the nose and out through the mouth, continue to breathe this way for a while.

(Pause 2mns)

At this point, your mind may start to wander and bring up random thoughts. Right now is not the time to worry, so gently guide your focus back to your breathing. Tell yourself that you will return to address those thoughts at a later date.

As you breathe deep and slow, focus all your attention on the breath. You can focus on how the air moves into your nose, passes your throat, and fills up your lungs or stomach. Make sure to give yourself a natural pause between the inhalation and the exhalation for the best experience.

Now, take a deep breath in…
And out…

At this point, you may allow your breathing to return to its natural rhythm. Your body will find the right rhythm on its own. You may notice that, at each breath you take, you are becoming more relaxed. With each exhale, imagine the tension in your body flying right out.

With each inhale, imagine breathing in deep relaxation, feeling more peaceful, more calm, more centered, with every breath.

Now, picture yourself standing close to a river, which is poured forth by a magnificent waterfall high above. You are in the middle of a forest. It is sunny and the sky is clear. It is not too hot or too cold.

In fact, though you are in the middle of, what seems to you, nowhere, you feel very much at ease. Somehow, this place feels very familiar and you do not know exactly where you are… Not just yet.

You sit down at the base of a tall tree, its leaves provide cool shades from the sun. You lay there, your back against the tree and your bottom supported by the soft and cool soil beneath. You let go of your body, feeling very relaxed and safe.

So while you are here, enjoy your time in this very beautiful and peaceful place. Sense this magical place with all your senses. Hear the cries of the wildlife that sang, only adding more to your relaxation. Listen to the water crashing down from the waterfall, its torrent flowing as true as your breathing. Take a few minutes now to enjoy your time in this place.

(Pause 3mns)

With the next exhale, let go. Let go. Allow the relaxation to happen to you, inviting it in of new your arms up to it welcoming it. It's so nice to be relaxed and it's so nice to even increase that relaxation by doubling it or tripling it and notice now how much extra relaxation you like at this very moment and breathing in.

As you breathe out, allowing that extra relaxation doubling or tripling it, to move through the body. Calm and relaxed. Soft and peaceful.

All the focus on letting go. The sound of my voice, nothing at all to do. Just follow the sound of my voice.

Very soon, we will work on melting away all the pain and soften the stiff muscles in your body. We will bring in the energy into all the right places, to direct it as you are in charge of your body. It can direct the healing energy wherever its most needed.

So let us begin by imagining that the air contains some healing properties. Let us give it a color, a vivid and radiant yellow, a symbol of positivity. Focus on its radiant beauty, its healing essence, and feel your body glow in this yellow at each breath you take. All that beautiful color, full of healing energy, full of tenderness, full of hope, full of prosperity.

Allow that color to move down into the body all the way down to a chest to the stomach so it sits in the core of the body and it radiates outwards. Perhaps it glows. Perhaps it vibrates.

Allow that healing energy a healing color to stay right there and yet it is becoming stronger and brighter and more powerful. Now, allow the mind to scan the whole body and find any spot where healing is required.

Moving your focus gently down your body from the top of your head to the tips of your toes now, finding any areas where your body is tense or stressed. But do not scrutinize. Allow your mind to guide you to that spot as the mind knows the body well, and the body also knows the mind well. Allow them to guide you on this healing process as they know what they need.

The mind will take you to those parts in the body that are damaged and are in pain that needs healing, some more than others. Find that first place and just watch. Just watch it through the mind's eye and notice the color, the shape, and you might notice that the area is more rigid. Perhaps more solid. It could be a block. Perhaps it's a bottleneck.

Whatever that tense area may feel or look like, when you finally find it, take a deep breath in. As you do so, feel that positive healing energy flowing into your body. Allow that energy to soak up in that tense area and erasing any signs of tension. Allow this radiant healing power to soothe that pain, that tension, or that stress. As you breathe out, feel the air that you exhale carrying away all that stress from your body, just like the flow of the river.

Continue to introduce this healing energy to the rest of your body until you are completely comfortable.

(Pause 2mns)

Now, it is time to finally relax the body thoroughly. On your next breath, feel your body absorbing all that healing positive energy. Imagine that your body is soaking up all that energy like a sponge and your body is glowing brighter and brighter, more radiant, more powerful. As you continue to breathe, feel your body sinking deeper and deeper into the state of relaxation.

You can repeat this process anywhere in the body by melting away the pain by bringing in that healing color, that loving energy, and making everything better, turning on all the cells in the area to heal and regenerate allowing that own pain to disappear permanently.

Just breathe in and out in a gentle rhythm as you do so.

(Pause 1 minute)

Your whole body now calm and relaxed. A beautiful peacefulness having flowed all through the body, through every muscle, and all old tension now has disappeared and that lovely and healing energy can fill the whole of the body.

Now, feel that energy flowing from the top of your head all the way to the tips of your toes. Feel this healing light radiating through your body. Feel this energy going through your legs and the hips, healing wounds all the way. From the shoulders to the arms, to the very tips of the fingers, through the whole of the chest and the neck, right up to the edge.

All in all, everything just gets better and better every day in every single way, healing and becoming stronger every day getting better and better as you care for yourself or look after yourself as you encourage this healing energy to flow to all the right places within you as you direct it.

As we come to the end of this meditation, picture yourself standing up again and gaze around at the magical place that you have been spending the last several minutes at.

Did you know that this is a place that your subconscious mind created? It knows exactly what is needed for you to heal. It knows exactly what your body and mind need. Now that you have visited this place consciously, you can return to this place again in the future.

All you have to do is to meditate and you will be transported back here, where nothing can harm your peace of mind.

Now, to conclude this meditation, I will count down from 5. As I do so, you will feel yourself returning to reality. Let us begin.

5… Slowly coming back now…

4… Feel your consciousness returning to your body…

3… Wiggle your toes now…

2… Take a deep breath…

1… Slowly open your eyes.

This concludes this meditation session. Thank you and have a nice day.

Easy to Follow Self-Healing Meditation (20mns)

Hello and welcome to this self-healing meditation. In this session, we will be working toward easing the pain and tension inside the body and allow you to rest comfortably. Self-healing meditation goes beyond just healing the body, but also the kind as well. If you are feeling hopeless, depressed, or stuck in a state of pain, then this quick self-healing meditation can help you shift your mindset to a more positive place.

First, get into a comfortable position, be it sitting or laying down. You may place your arms and legs however you like so long as you are comfortable. You will be here for quite a while, after all. As this meditation is intended to ease any tension within the body and mind, it pays to remain in a comfortable position.

If at any point in this session, you feel any discomfort from staying still, you may move a bit to ease that pain and you can return to this meditation seamlessly.

Right now, you don't have to close your eyes yet. You don't have to focus on anything. Just let the mind go about on its business and your eyes gazing at random things in your room.

Right now, you just want to tell the body and mind to relax. So go ahead and take a deep breath to let the body and mind know that it is time to unwind. Take another deep breath now and allow yourself to sink further into the state of relaxation.

In… And out…
In… And out…
In… And out…

Excellent. If you haven't done so already, go ahead and close your eyes now. Slowly do so and let your vision fade to black. Inhale deeply and exhale completely. Allow your body to relax and to be still. Let your muscles soften and let your muscles lengthen.

On your next breath, breathe in through your nose, hold it at the top for a few seconds and then exhale slowly. As you hold your breath, focus on the stillness in the air and your body and mind. Focus on what that stillness feels like.

Remember what it feels like as we will spread its tranquility toward the rest of the body and mind.

Now, let us work on relaxing the body. We will do a simple body scan exercise. Simply shift your focus from your breathing to the top of your head, and move it slowly down your body until you reach the tips of your toes.

As you do so, notice any sensations that you feel. Gently pay attention. Some areas may already be relaxed. Some might be tense. If you notice any areas of tension or discomfort, simply take notice of where they are as we will come back to them later.

Let go of any judgment. Just be aware and sensitive to the messages of your body. Now bring your focus to your breathing. Notice the depth and notice the pace of every inhale and every exhale, allow your breath to become slower and softer.

Take a deep inhale through your nose and a long exhale through your mouth. Try that again. Deep inhale through your nose… And long exhale through your mouth.

Feel every breath flowing through your body as you inhale and as you exhale, stay connected to the sensations of your body.

At this point, your mind may start to wander and bring up random thoughts. Some of them might be worrying. Some are pleasant. Whatever those thoughts are, simply acknowledge their presence. Maybe you could remain with them for a few seconds, but no longer. Push them aside and guide your focus back to your breathing, using it to anchor yourself to the present moment.

Now, give your body permission to relax and to let go breathe in love and breathe out tension. Breathe in peace and breathe out negativity. Breathe and healing, breathe out hurt. Stay focused on this breath.

Allow your body to soften breathe in love, breathe out tension.

Using your breath as an anchor, focus on that stillness between your inhale and exhale. Observe it and understand its power. Use the healing power of your breathing and introduce that stillness to any part of the body that is hurt or tense.

Scan through your body once more and when you find that area of tension, focus on that area, and breathe deeply and intensely. Allow the breath to sweep away that tension like a gentle yet powerful tide that takes all the negative energy from your body.

Continue to do this for a few minutes or until your body is thoroughly relaxed.

(Pause 3mns)

Now let us work on cleansing the mind of that negative energy. As you breathe, introduce all that positive energy to the mind. Breathe in positivity, breathe out negativity.

Breathe in rejuvenation, breathe out tension.
Breathe in self-love, breathe out self-loathing.
Breathe in love, breathe out stress.
Breathe in peace, breathe out chaos.

Allow your body to be still and to be silent. Let your body and mind do the job. All you have to do is breathe deeply. They will do the rest. They will heal what needs to be healed.

With every breath, allow yourself to relax further and deeper. Allow this feeling of relaxation and calm to spread throughout your whole body feel the sense of peace wash over you.

Be here right now. Every cell in your body knows how to heal itself your body is always working towards perfect health.

Choose to release any and all obstacles to healing, choose to wash your thinking, and think only healthy, loving thoughts. Choose to love your body and send love to every organ, bone, muscle, and part of your body.

Now flood every cell of your body with love. Choose to be grateful to your body. Choose to accept healing and good health.

Now take a deep breath. This concludes this healing meditation.

Guided Sleep Meditation (20mns)

Hello and welcome to this guided sleep meditation. In this session, you will go on a journey of deep relaxation after a long day of work when you just want to unwind and have a restful sleep.

To begin, make sure that all distractions are as minimal as possible. As you progress, anything holding you back from fully relaxing will slowly start to fade away. Lay in a position that is comfortable for you. Allow yourself to go deeper and experience a willing openness to the sleep that you should be getting.

Please leave all thoughts about yourself behind and anything that has caused worry or stress. It may be easier said than done but just place it to the back of your mind for now.

Focus on my voice and the words that you hear will give clarity to unfold your mind for sleep.

If you are ready and willing to be present at this moment, your journey into a deep relaxing and pleasing sleep will begin.

As you lay there in a gentler awareness of observation, noticing how your body is laid, sense, and feel any areas soften to a looseness that promotes a sleepier state.

Now, breathe in deeply and exhale fully.

Breathe in deeply...

And exhale fully...

Allow the sound of your breathing to soothe and calm your mind and soul.

Breathe in deeply...

And exhale fully...

You may notice that thoughts and internal mental chatters are happening inside your mind.

This is fine.

This is completely normal.

These thoughts will begin to quiet down as you concentrate on listening to your own breathing.

As you listen to your inhale, you will find your mind gently begin to quiet down.

So, breathe in deeply, taking in the cool and refreshing air

And exhale fully, pushing out hot and tense air.

You may feel your body starting to loosen up and relaxing as you allow the sound of your own breathing to soothe your soul, taking in the infinite source of energy within you.

Just through breathing alone, you allow yourself to be in total peace with your surroundings.

Now, take the time to scan your entire body, noticing any areas of tension. Focus your breathing on those areas, starting from your toes and moving up to the top of your head. Work on one area at a time.

Breathe deep and slow, allowing your breath to soothe any tension in your muscles.

(Pause 5mns)

Now that your entire body is fully relaxed, take another breath to allow your body to slip more and more into a relaxed state.

Feel how at ease your mind and body are. Feel the relief and benefit of letting go of any worries that were on your thoughts…

Going into an even deeper, sleepier, and more relaxed state, let the visualization of any thoughts begin to fade off in the darkness behind your eyelids, drifting deeper into a transitioning positive dream and sleep…

As you sleep, your body rests, healing as you recuperate and regenerate positive energy in every muscle fiber and cell of yourself.

Sleeping keeps your mind and body muscle memory to remember that when you sleep well, you can do it again. Let go of anything holding you back and truly allow yourself to relax through letting go.

Your mind has the space to rationalize every thought to a groundedness of truth and ones that only benefits you as the person you are on the inside.

Allow yourself to be more at ease with each and every thought that passes your mind. Any tension from this moment on that is caused by our worry or a stressor in your life is quickly brought to a reasonable place. See it for what it truly is before manifesting itself in your body.

You are not the manifestation of such worrying thoughts, so dismiss them with positive self-love that only nourishes your mind and body better.

As you begin and continue to let go of anything negative, you will find that you become more relaxed, calmer, and more at peace within everything.

Going deeper every muscle now, descending more as you slip into an even sleepier state. Knowing that you have more control over how you reason with your mind allows you to go deeper, no sound from the outside can be heard, no light except the positivity inside you that shines, and a feeling of touch is but now a softness of comfort.

Resting, heavily breathing deeply, you just let go. The touch of the sheets beneath you begin to fade away. The sensation of your own vibrations and internal energy are the only things you can sense.

Everything is being replaced with a positive and healing feeling of peace inside. There is no need to think about anything right now. Now is a time for sleep and only sleep. It's the one thing that will replenish you every night as you lay there.

Feel the vibration of positivity growth around your whole body. You may see it as a distant colored light behind your eyelids or a feeling of tingling in your hands or toes, warmer and heavier with each and every noticeably relaxing breath that you take, every inhalation of oxygen only sends you deeper into a space of contentedness and peace. The sense of relief is immense and far-reaching into the deep thoughts of your mind.

Healing any bad feeling you have of yourself. Only positive thoughts can be experienced in this moment and every moment onwards allowing you to drift heavier and warmly into it refreshing deep sleep.

As you sleep the defense mechanism only grows to protect you from negativity. You feel it as a glowy warm feeling around your heart or chest area, growing in strength as you sleep, feeling more positive with every second that passes.

From this moment on you only sleep a positive sleep. You only rest and relax more easily and from this moment on, you find it easier to drift off, feeling the relief of letting go of every aspect of today, leaving it all behind to be nourished and filled with only positivity in every sense of your inner being.

Rest now. Relax more, and just let go.

Stress Relief Meditation (30mns)

Hello and welcome to this stress relief meditation. This meditation is designed to help you relax and be as calm as you can. So go ahead and get into a comfortable position, be it sitting or laying down. Whatever works for you so long as you are comfortable, which is important for a fruitful meditation session.

Next, take a deep breath. You do not even have to close your eyes or focus on anything in particular. You can let your eyes and mind roam as much as they please. For now, all you have to do is to just breathe deeply and let your body and mind unwind and relax.

Breathe in… And out…
In… and out…
In... And out…

Excellent. Now, when you inhale, slowly close your eyes and open them again as you exhale. Continue to do this for a minute or so or until your eyes become heavy. If they do become heavy, you may go ahead and close them.

(Pause 1mn)

Good. Your eyes should start to feel very heavy right now, so go ahead and close them if you haven't already and shift your focus to your breathing.

As you continue to breathe, observe how it feels, how the air enters and exits your body. Study how the air flows throughout your body in all its essence.

(Pause 1mn)

On your next breath in, take a deep breath through your nose and hold it at the top for a few seconds before you let it out through the mouth. This time, focus on that gentle stillness in the air as you hold your breath. Again, observe what it feels like and all of its essence. Continue to do this for another minute or so.

(Pause 1mn)

Excellent. Now, you may allow your breath to return to its natural rhythm. As you listen to my voice, your body may begin to relax more and more. Trust that your body can find its best way to let go naturally. You cannot force relaxation.

Maybe that your body needs to heal in other ways. It's good to know that your unconscious mind is an expert in healing and balancing in a safe and natural way while you can just flow with the experience.

Now, take a few deep breaths...

In... And out...

Continue to do this until your body sinks deeper into relaxation.

(Pause 1mn)

Become aware of your breathing. Imagine now that you're breathing in that life energy through the soles of your feet, breathing it up through your body, and breathe it out the top of your head. Continue to breathe and feel this flow of energy...

(Pause 1mn)

There is no right the wrong way to flow with this experience. Just breathe and relax, feeling the life energy flowing through you…

(Pause 2mns)

Feel the deep sense of comfort as you breathe…

(Pause 1mn)

If at any point during this session, your mind starts to wander, simply guide it back to your breathing. No need to beat yourself up for it because it is natural for the mind to wander and bring up random thoughts sometimes.

There is no need to stress about it. Just acknowledge that the thought is there and tell yourself that you will return to address those thoughts at a later time. Tell yourself that now is the time to relax, not stress about anything. There is a time and place for everything and right here, right now is not the time to feel any negativity. Now is the time for self-care and self-love, that which you truly deserve.

As you acknowledge this fact, you might already be starting to chip away any worry, fear, and stress in the subconscious mind. This will continue with every second in every minute of every breath.

Now, imagine yourself walking on a warm beach. Imagine walking so close to the sea that some of the waves touch your feet. As the waves come crashing in on the shore, synchronize your breath with them. The waves coming in is your inhaling, and the waves fading out back to sea as you exhale. Feel the waves washing away your troubled thoughts.

This is your safe haven. This is a beautiful place formed by the power of the subconscious mind. It knows that this place brings relaxation to the body and mind and it created that just for you.

As you wander this place, know that this is your safe place. It is safe for you to let go of all your worldly worries. Now, picture the sun above you glowing bright yet emit a gentle healing aura and bathing your body with its divine power. Feel yourself glowing with this radiant light, feel its energy surging through your body, and filling you with a peaceful silence.

This quietness flows through your veins permeating every cell in your body.

Feel every atom every molecule of your body, mind, and spirit allowing yourself to be healed and balanced, becoming very aware of that deep sense of peacefulness inside you.

As you do so and I'll leave you in silence for a few moments as your body, mind, heart, and spirit continue the process of letting go and heal.

(Pause 2mn)

Now, you are calm. You feel calm and balanced. This sense of calm, control and balance will continue to grow stronger and stronger every day, more and more, as you meditate and reinforce these positive energies within you.

You're doing good. You are taking control of your mind, body, and emotions. You are feeling better and better, feeling calm, harmonious, and relaxed at all times.

That calmness, that inner peace is growing and spreading through and around your body. As you continue to relax the things in life that were not giving you a positive experience now, they seem to calm you now.

They seem to make you stronger now. They seem to connect you with your inner strengths and power.

Whatever you experience in life, you are better than that. You choose to show up in your life and honor the opportunity that you have been given.

You are a pure life force in the human body. You are worthy

Imagine that you start walking forwards along the beach leaving footprints in the sand the Sun still beaming its powerful celestial energy upon your being.

You feel surprisingly freer. Imagine that every step every footprint represents patterns that are not supportive of your intention to live your full potential and it is safe for you to let go now so you walk steadily and courageously towards your new future.

After a while, you turn around maybe you notice that your footprints are being washed away by the waves. Your first steps are gone now washed away

Let go now and it is safe and you're doing good. For each step you take, the lighter and freer you feel walking more and more effortlessly towards your new future much freer.

Ahead of you, there is a person approaching. It is you. It is you one month from now.

Notice how relaxed your future self feels. Notice how good your future self feels that balanced energy is emanating from your future self over there.

Your future self comes towards you and gives you the warmest most compassionate hug that you have felt in a long time. All that love unconditionally flowing between you. The effect of this positivity will be reinforced in your dreams, compounded in your sleep. You'll wake up tomorrow feeling marvelous, looking forward to another great day in your life.

You feel confident to do all the things you want to do it's getting easier and easier and situations that used to bother you now just seemed to make you stronger.

They seem to connect you with your inner power and it's getting easier and easier.

You feel calm, strong, confident, and relaxed each day as you become increasingly more able to let go and relax so you feel a sense of calmness, a sense of peacefulness growing inside you.

This growing feeling of inner calmness, quiet, confidence, is sufficient to reassure you that as each day passes, you are more and more becoming the person you'd like to be. The ideal for you. The authentic you. You are worthy. You are a believer in yourself. You're more than good enough. You are valuable. You are important. You are worthy. You're more than good enough. You are courageous and you stand up for yourself because you choose to be you. You are flexible to changes happening in your life.

The more accepting you are to change, the easier it feels. Change is a natural aspect of life. It is a sign of life and you choose life.

You are a beautiful expression of life. You breathe easily in a relaxed way and you detach more and more from the earthly drama that's going on around us.

You can begin to experience a greater and greater sense of joy in your life now and as each day passes, you become happier healthier, and more fulfilled and totally at ease in yourself.

You are safe. You accept that you are you.

All these words are vibrating at the frequency of truth and because all of this begin to happen now.

You begin to feel much happier much more content, much more optimistic, much more positive in every way. You radiate goodness. The future you and then now you embrace one more time this time becoming one.

When you feel ready and decide to open your eyes you will bring with you this positive radiant energy that emanates from within you. Your inner light shines stronger and brighter than ever.

You may be surprised by how calm strong and content you feel in the hours days weeks and months ahead. All is well.

Calming After a Panic Attack Meditation (20mns)

Hello and welcome to this guided calming meditation. In this session, we will be working toward relaxing the mind and body. The fact that you are here means that you had just gone through a rather unfortunate and stressful situation. We will work to repair the damage that the event has caused so that you may return to your day, feeling better.

So, go ahead and get into a comfortable position, be it laying down or sitting up. We will be here for a while, so you want to be as comfortable as possible. During this session, if you ever feel any discomfort, you may move your body a bit to ease that discomfort.

Without further ado, close your eyes if you haven't already. As you do so, focus on your breathing, how the air enters and exits your body. Take a deep breath to tell the body and mind that it is time to slow down, to tell them that there is no need to go anywhere or think about anything.

Tell yourself that you are right where you want to be. Now is the time to unwind and relax. You are safe here. Nothing can harm you here. Nothing can take away the inner peace and tranquility within you. So take another deep breath now and let that peace and tranquility seep out of your subconscious mind, and bathing the body and mind with its magical aura.

Take a deep breath in through your nose, holding it at the top for 2 or 3 seconds, and then breathe out through your mouth. As you do so, focus on that gentle stillness between your inhale and exhale. Observe it in all its essence and introduce it to every inch of your being. Allow this gentle stillness or peace to soothe and calm the body and mind.

Remain with your breath and breathe like this for a few minutes.

(Pause 3mns)

Excellent. You may continue to breathe as you normally would now. At this point, your mind may start to wander and it might randomly bring up various thoughts that make you feel different things. It might bring up pleasant thoughts, which may make you smile.

It might bring up unpleasant thoughts, which may displease you. Some negative thoughts might be about the things that caused you so much distress in the first place.

Right now is not the time to think, so if your mind does wander, simply guide it back to your breathing, using your breath as an anchor to hold it in the present moment. Focus on the stillness in the air and the gentle flow of your breathing.

Relax…

Nothing here can harm you…

All will be well…

Things might look bad for you, but if you return to it with a clear head, you can solve any problem. Nothing is impossible. Just give your body and mind enough time and space and they will help you achieve your purpose…

Maybe you are worrying too much. Maybe you are trying to control things that are completely out of your control. Maybe luck just wasn't in your favor.

Whatever the case may be, the fact that you felt the way you did was valid. All feelings are valid and you need to acknowledge that. But remaining in that stressful situation is not the way to go. You need to have a clear mind so that you can make the right decisions and make the best out of the situation.

To do this, you need to relax... Unwind and relax... Take a deep breath now to remind your body and mind to relax. Right now is not the time for worry. You will come back to your duties at a later time.

Without moving your body, surrender everything to the universe around you. Let go of everything and let the universe support your entire being. Unwind and let go, allowing the surface beneath you to support your body.

Welcome the universe with open arms and tell yourself that the universe is kind and loving. If it is not kind and loving, why do such things feel so pleasant in the first place? You are a child of the universe, and the universe loves you just like a loving parent would.

It is not here to harm you. It is here to heal you. Simply let go and welcome its presence with open arms. Allow it to hold you, to cradle you, to give you positivity. Things may not go the way you want them to, but that might be because the universe got something even better planned for you. Trust in the universe and you can never go wrong.

Take a moment now and smile to yourself, for you chose to go through this session and experience the love that grows within you as we speak. Thank yourself for giving yourself time and space to unwind and relax, so that you can go back out there with a clear head and a calm mind.

As we come to the end of this session, take another deep breath and open your eyes whenever you are ready to take on the world once more. With the entire universe behind your back, all your endeavors will succeed.

Thank you and good luck with your journey.

Deep Relaxation Meditation (20mns)

Hello and welcome to this deep relaxation meditation. In this session, we will be working toward relaxing both the body and mind.

Let us begin by going to a distraction-free place and getting into a comfortable position. You can either sit or lie down and place your arms and legs however you want. You will be here for quite some time so it is important that you remain as comfortable as possible. Relaxation cannot be achieved without comfort, after all.

Once you are ready, you don't have to close your eyes yet. Just follow my voice and take a deep breath now.

Excellent. Again.

In… And out…
In… And out…
In… And out…

Excellent. Now, continue to breathe for another while. You can let your mind and eyes wander as they please for now. Just continue to breathe normally and allow the mind and body to sink deeper into the state of relaxation. During this time, if you feel the need to close your eyes, you may go ahead and close them.

(Pause 1mn)

If you haven't done so already, go ahead and close your eyes now. As your vision fades to black, shift your focus to your own breathing. Take another deep breath through the nose, and out through the mouth.

Now, let us work on soothing the pain in your body. To do this, simply shift your focus to the top of your head and gradually move your focus down to the rest of your body.

Starting with the forehead now. Loosen the muscles in that area… Allow them to lengthen and relax… Let your eyebrows settle into their natural position. You might be squeezing your eyes. Allow them to relax.

Surrender to this tranquil darkness that surrounds. Surrender to the universe around you and know that you will be well taken care of.

Moving slowly down now. Allow your tongue to rest in its natural position. Allow your jaw to loosen. Allow all muscles of your head to soften, unwind, and relax.

There is nothing you need to do right now but to breathe and relax…

Moving down to your torso now… Relax those shoulders… Feel your arms becoming limp… Feel your fingers unfurling or curling up into their natural positions. Feel your arms loosening up… Feel your stomach moving up as you inhale, and down as you exhale. Feel the air entering and exiting your body as you breathe… Relax your entire torso…

Moving further down now to your legs… Again… No need to tense up any areas… Just let those muscles relax and unwind. Breathe deeply and allow that air to just wash away all the tension in your body… Feel your legs becoming soft and heavy, fully relaxed in the present moment.

Now, scan through your body again and notice any areas that are either tense or uncomfortable. We will now work on relaxing those areas as well.

Imagine that the air has the healing property that your body and mind need. Imagine that it is a golden healing aura. On your next breath, picture this glowing aura flowing into your body, infusing its healing energy to rejuvenate the body. Feel your body glowing softly as it soaks up all that positive energy. Allow your body to take whatever it needs to repair itself.

You have been working hard, you know? You might not have taken nearly enough care of yourself. Even so, you recognize the importance of self-care and self-love. You might be too busy in the past that you did not give yourself enough love or care.

But the fact that you are here, giving your body and mind the time and space they need to relax, is a sign that you indeed cherish the body that you are given. It is a sign that you do love yourself and that you are treating yourself the way you treat a loved one. That is what is called self-love – treating yourself like someone you love and care for. This love alone is so valuable that nothing even comes close to it.

The fact that you are taking care of yourself now is a gift, from you to yourself. It is a very beautiful gift. So, smile now in gratitude to yourself for you chose to take care of yourself. You choose to take care of your needs first so that you could function at your best.

If, at any point during this session, your mind starts to wander, simply remain with your thoughts for a few seconds. But do not linger for too long as some thoughts may provoke certain emotions and it will not do to get caught in those emotions right now.

There is a time and place for everything. Now is not the time to be worried, scared, anxious, or angry. Now is the time for the mind and body to relax.

As you continue to breathe and bathe in this beautiful healing aura, use the power of your focus to direct that energy and guide it to areas where you feel tense or pain. Allow your breathing to wash away all the pain and tension from your body. Allow the healing aura to go to that area, to repair, to rejuvenate, to heal those wounded areas, so that you may sink deeper and deeper into relaxation.

As we come to the close of this meditation, take another deep breath and count slowly down from 10. As I do so, feel your consciousness returning to your body.

10… Slowly coming back…

9…

8… Feel your consciousness returning to your body…

7…

6… Slowly wiggle your toes and fingers…

5…

4… Take a deep breath now…

3… Once more…

2… Coming back now…

1… You have returned.

Thank you.

Adult Bedtime Story 1 (60mns)

Thomas is startled as he awakens abruptly. He had nearly dozed off, his head having fallen backward to rest on the wall behind him. Thomas looks around and notices that he is not the only one.

All around him, early morning workers are catching a few more moments of sleep before arriving at their destinations, though no one else seems to have awoken at that moment.

"Must be one of those hypnotic jerks," he thinks, "Perhaps I hadn't even fallen asleep at all."

Thomas's daily commute is a particularly long one. He lives in his own flat at the southernmost end of the Northern Line in London. Despite the lengthy journey into work each morning, he never misses an opportunity to remind himself of how grateful he is to find an open seat. He is always one of the first on the train.

Perhaps he thinks the distance is worth the seated journey and Thomas think about the place he is whizzing off to at the early hour in the day. Thomas is a program manager for a small but well-respected software development company based in London. He has worked there for nearly eight years, having started there when he first finished his studies.

He enjoys the company of the people he works with and has a good working relationship with his boss but something in Thomas's gut contracts each time he thinks about walking into the office.

He watches this reaction come and then watches it leave though never forgetting that something is not sitting right. He arrives at work that morning and says hello to the others who have also arrived at 7:00 a.m. He prefers to get his day started as soon as possible so that he can finish up early and enjoy the late day sun as it falls upon the lush green parks of London.

His fingers get to work, typing away to clients, and working on projects. Sometimes, when the afternoon rolls around and the others have not yet returned from lunch, he takes a break from software to do some research on places he might like to visit.

Maybe Japan Australia or Greece. But on this particular morning, he is focused he's busy working on a new project for a startup company based in Athens. As he types away, his boss gently interrupts him with a proposal.

"Thomas I've been thinking," she says, "I had really loved for us to get to know the team in Athens on a personal level. I'd like to send you over there to meet our clients and to put a face to our name. There really is potential here for a long and strong relationship the first time in a long time."

Thomas beams and his heart flutters, a smile stretched from ear to ear. His boss, Louisa, takes this as a yes.

He'll spend five days in the city with plenty of time for both work and a bit of exploration. Thomas's mother is Greek, having grown up just outside of Athens. Many months ago, she moved to England when she was quite young returning only a few times.

Since then, Thomas himself has never been but has always felt a strong yearning in his bones to return to the place of his ancestors. Life has simply gotten too busy. He knows that this is no excuse and later that night, Thomas begins packing with glee.

Though he is not due to leave until the end of the week, Thomas struggles to contain his excitement, and understandably so. He calls his mother and father to tell them about his business trip. They were very delighted.

Thomas rests in his bed that night, looking out his window to the stars and the sky. The moon is nearly full, illuminating the city and the surrounding lands below. Planes pass by as flashing lights that effortlessly float across the universe.

Thomas thought to himself that he will soon be on such a magical vessel. He has not flown since he was a teenager and he is now approaching 30. Memories begin creeping into his mind. He thinks about his childhood and the strong bond he had with his grandparents.

His grandfather on his father's side was a farmer. Thomas remembers running through the fields with him and sometimes into the forest to collect wild berries and herbs. He always felt as if he was in a fairy tale when they wandered off into the woods.

Something about it felt mystical. Perhaps it was the way the wind would rustle the leaves or the sounds of the fluttering birds. Perhaps it was the crunching or tweaks underfoot. He loved the smell of evergreens and the way the light trickled in through the dense canopy overhead.

Perhaps he thinks it was a blend of all these things. Thomas remembers vividly the way his mother cooked, the way she laughed. The incredibly kind and loving mother he always knew and loved. Thomas remembers that he and his sister, Katrina, would help in the kitchen wherever they could. The two of them would rinse and dry the leafy greens and herbs and then help their grandmother cook the pasta sauce. They would stir, and stir, and stir as she added all sorts of aromatic herbs to the simmering tomatoes. Maybe that was how he was such a great cook today.

It has been a long time since Thomas had cooked. This realization stirred something in his belly. He missed it. He missed the slowness of time that enveloped him when he helped his grandmother prepare dinner.

It's been too long far too long. He thinks at this moment. Thomas vows to get back into the kitchen after returning from his trip to Athens. The week passes slowly until finally, Friday arrives.

With his bags packed, Thomas takes one last look around his apartment. He knows he's only gone for an extra-long weekend, but says "so long" anyways. While on the train to the airport, Thomas admires the greenery of London's outskirts.

The sun is shining and the May blossoms are a sure sign that spring has arrived. He feels quiet anticipation whirling in his heart. The trip is primarily for business, but he will have the entire weekend to explore the city of Athens before meeting his client on Monday.

It has been a long time since he has taken a trip like this and one to his mother's homeland is stirring his sense of adventure. His flight to Athens from London is only a few hours long. The plane soars through the clouds. Thomas looks down on the continent below appearing and disappearing as the plane moves in and out of the skies.

Thomas thinks how miraculous it is that humans are able to fly. As a child, he often dreamt about being able to fly. One particular reoccurring dream, he would watch himself sprout wings and soar across open fields and oceans.

He'd been awake, thinking that perhaps the dream was a prophecy for his future. Thomas laughs to himself at the recognition of this memory and thinks perhaps this sort of flying is not quite the same. Even so, it is certainly close enough.

The plane lands by early afternoon and Thomas makes his way into the center of town. He's staying at a small guesthouse within a short walking distance of the city's ancient ruins. He checks in and wanders up the spiral stone staircase to the third floor.

His room is immaculate with a delicate blend of rustic and modern touches. It is simple but it is all he could need. He takes a deep breath in and releases a sigh as he breathes out a wave of peace and comfort overcomes him.

A small balcony with sheer curtains covering the glass door that opens to the outside world. Thomas makes his way to the balcony and steps out his room looks out into the ancient acropolis. Athens buzzes below, a city ready to explore.

Thomas wanders through the narrow streets and alleys through markets and along winding roads that are lined with trees. With no map he feels entirely lost and yet, with no concerns in the world, he is taking the unknown road, allowing it to unfold as he goes step by step.

He takes a few set of stairs and wanders along cobblestone pathways until he reaches the foot of the Acropolis, staring up at this ancient fortress Thomas feels for a moment as if he is wandered back in time.

He wonders what it would have been like to live in ancient Greece. Countless myths come to mind as he recalls some of the stories his grandmother used to tell. He remembers feeling so very otherworldly, like the way being at the foot of the Acropolis feels to him now.

He pays his admission and ventures in, finding his breath having gone missing for just a few moments as he enters. Something has taken him aback, nearly moving him to tears. He surrenders to this space and to the emotion arising in him.

He realizes how long it has been since he allowed himself the trip to Athens. Thomas sees a version of himself that he can't quite describe but one that brings about feelings of peace, confidence, and clarity.

He breathes in and out effortlessly as he wanders the ancient Greek city. He dedicates the entire weekend to simply indulging in local cuisine, breathing in the history of ancient ruins, and sleeping soundly for as long as his body calls for.

All worries melt away as he grants himself permission to be entirely present with the land whose history courses through his veins. It has been a long time since he has slept so well.

He drifts off easily and awakes, feeling inspired and energized as he explores. He somehow forgets all about his meeting on Monday morning. But still, when the morning arrives, he packs his computer and heads to the startup small office in the center of town.

Thomas meets with Sam, the company's founder, and is introduced to the team he's been working with virtually over the past month. They talk about all things tech for what feels like hours.

Meanwhile, Thomas's heart is elsewhere. The meeting wraps up and Sam thanks him greatly for coming all the way to Athens to see what the company is like on the ground level. Thomas smiles and thanks him in return and heads back to his hotel for the final evening.

A mixture of emotions brews inside of him but he struggles to put his finger on what his heart is calling for on his final night in the city. Thomas sits on his balcony overlooking the ruins and the rest of the city.

The air is warm and the sky is clear, not a cloud covers the sky. The moon now waxing still casts a strong glow across the Earth's surface below. Thomas gazes up at it, feeling a vaguely familiar connection to the stars and the moon many years ago.

Thomas recalls being by the sea with his parents and his sister. Each summer, they would pack up the car and drive to a small bed-and-breakfast in the southwest tip of England. The days during these long summer weekends were slow, time was spent walking along the beach or wandering nearby towns and villages.

Evenings were early but Thomas remembers that on some warm nights, his father would prepare hot chocolate and fill a couple of cups to the brim. The family would sit beneath the stars, pointing out the few constellations they knew, at the same time sipping the sweet summer treat out of their travel mugs.

Now, Thomas feels nostalgia washing over him. Nostalgia for the days when he had fewer worries and was more connected to the natural world around him. He stares up at the moon now, feeling a wave of peace and comfort come over him as if it were a lullaby.

The moon overtakes him, offering a sense that it is now time to rest his body. It is now time to let his body sleep for the night. Thomas makes his way to his bed and dozes off swiftly and soundly.

Thomas returns to London the next day. Over the next few days, he feels a strong longing for something though he's not quite sure for what. He has a clear sense that it has something to do with his trip to Athens.

He misses the way that adventure made him feel it was as though a part of him was coming up to the surface, coming back to his conscious awareness senses that something is calling for his attention, but he's not quite sure what to make of it or what exactly it is saying.

Thomas struggles to focus on his work over the coming weeks. The voice is growing but he's starting to fear it. He wonders if it would have been easier had he never gone to Athens at all. He knows that something in him now is questioning the life he is living, but it feels too frightening to listen more closely to that voice.

It appears he has no choice. The whispers become louder and louder until finally becoming clear and confident. It told them with confidence that he should return to the roots.

He's not quite sure where the path will lead him though he knows one thing for certain. He must leave his job and return to the place that inspired him. He must return to the country that changed things.

Fear brews in his belly. He is not one for taking risks, preferring to take pathways that are safe and well-lit. He knows that he needs to jump. He knows that now is the time to take a risk. His future self, whoever that may be, is depending on it.

Thomas resigns, spending the next two weeks tying up loose ends and passing projects on to other team members. He prepares himself for the unknown. He thinks back to a quote by Lord Byron that he first heard some time ago. It reads:

"There is pleasure in the pathless woods by divine grace."

His sister returns to London from the United States to take over his apartment while he ventures back to the land their ancestors come from, unsure of where he is going. Thomas closes his eyes and places his finger on a map of Greece islands included to decide which road to take.

It lands on a faraway island in the Aegean Sea, on the small remote island. He books flights to reach this unknown land and packs his bags. Though he is not sure how long he will be gone for, he knows it will be at least a few months.

He's ready to reset entirely, not quite knowing what that means. He finds a small guesthouse online offering long-term accommodation and books for two months to start. It located high up in the mountains, in a small village, and with plenty of gardens around the property. It sounds just like what he's looking for

The plane lands a few days later in the south end of the island. Thomas calls a taxi that takes him to a small guesthouse in the tiny village of Menendez, a small town that overlooks the stretch of sea between Greece and Turkey. The owners of the small apartment he is renting lived just next door and come out to greet him they welcome him with open arms, showing him around the grounds that will be his home for the next few months.

They extend an offer for him to join them at dinner. Thomas unpacks his belongings and stares out the window that overlooks the surrounding mountains and the port below in the fresh mountain air.

He cracks open the window. he's not quite sure what he is doing here he knows he's in the right place. Thomas heads for the hills, packing a small bag with water and fruit to sustain him for the afternoon's adventure.

He walks through the mountains admiring the vastness of this small island. Low-lying shrubs blanket the land as red yellow and magenta blossoms brighten the primal landscape. The sun beams down from overhead as he walks, allowing his instinct to guide him.

He wanders the land with no plan, and no goal to guide him. He realizes it's been years since he'd walked this aimlessly perhaps not since childhood. He feels free, completely untethered, and prepared to begin again.

He had expected to be overcome with jitters during these first few days, but he feels quite at peace. Instead, occasionally, worried thoughts overcome his mind, hounding him with questions about what his plan is and what his intentions are. Though he knows that he does not hold the answers to these questions just yet, he reminds himself that that is okay.

Upon his return to the apartment, he witnesses how tired his body feels. He finds Maria and George, the owners of the guest house, and politely asks if he might join them the following night for dinner instead as he's feeling tired from the day's activity. They tell him to rest well and let him know that he is welcome to join them anytime.

Thomas slips quietly into bed and falls swiftly into a deep, deep sleep. That night, he dreams that he is an astronaut, floating far away in outer space looking down at the world and realizing how small it really is from way out in the galaxy. The earth feels like a very small home.

He realizes it is just one planet amongst millions of other floating bodies in the universe. This dream brings him a sense of wonder, inspiration, and a newfound appreciation for the earth he lives on and for the life that courses through his body.

From way up here, he can see that the earth is a home amongst other homes, and in the dream, he thinks, "Wow what a beautiful home I ended up living in."

Thomas awakens the next morning, feeling the clarity of the dream still with him, and in honor of the earth, he decides to walk yet again. He connects with the earth through each step he takes.

Somehow, Thomas feels as if he is a baby learning to walk for the first time. He's never given much thought to the ground beneath his feet but now he feels deeply connected to the land that supports him.

After some time, he reaches a secluded beach where he nestles himself into the warm sand. He revels at the way the sand seems to wrap itself around his body as he nestles in. Staring out at the ocean, he is reminded of the dream and of how the Earth revolves around as one complete unit.

In his bones, he now knows that he and everything around him lives and breathes together as a single organism. He breathes in the ocean air, feeling more and more settled in.

That afternoon, Thomas returns to the guesthouse feeling more energized and connected to himself and to the land. He makes his way to the second building on the property, to the home occupied by Maria and George, getting ready for dinner by chopping herbs, rolling small pieces of pasta, and preparing their home-baked bread.

He watches how intuitively their hands work with the food they are preparing and offers to help.

"I won't be as quick as you," he warns them, to which they reply, "Speed is not a desirable factor in our kitchen. If anything, we like when things move slowly,"

Thomas's reminded me of how things moved in his grandmother's kitchen and feels right at home. Over the next few days, Maria and George teach Thomas how to prepare local delicacies using herbs and produce from the land.

Along the way, it dawns on him. He has lost himself entirely to the kitchen, lost to the state of flow. His hands begin to work with the food and he prepares more effortlessly and intuitively.

Thomas is reminded of how much joy real food brings him. One night during his first week, he has another vivid dream. This time, however, he is in an open meadow. Beneath a large awning, wooden tables are lined up beneath the canopy and are adorned with lace tablecloths and freshly picked flowers.

Small twinkling lights lined the edges of the awning as dusk falls. His loved ones make their way to the table. Thomas stands at the head of the table and passes down dish after dish of food he has prepared for his friends and family. The group feasts, laughing and whispering beneath the midsummer night sky, savoring the head chef's succulent creations.

In the morning he awakes, knowing exactly what he is here for. He thinks about the voice that came to him just a few weeks ago that whispered, "Get back to the roots," and suddenly it becomes clear.

The roots he was meant to rediscover were not only the roots that connected him to Greece, but also those that permeate the land. He wants to know the earth through food. He wants to nourish the earth and the people on it through preparing wholesome plant foods and living in connection to the land.

He finds Maria that morning and joins her in the garden as he roams the rows of plants. He feels inspired to learn about each one, to get to know the way they grow. He asks Maria if she might teach him everything she knows and she beams. She would be honored to pass on her knowledge of the land.

Thomas remains on this little yet vibrant island for six more months, soaking up every bit of wisdom he can get. His heart and soul poured on to take care of the soil, to harvest, to forage, to cook.

When his final month in Greece comes around, he feels prepared to bring his knowledge back to his more permanent home of London and to begin his life again. Thomas's last morning in Greece, he wakes early in heads to his favorite trail through the mountains. The Sun has not yet risen and there are no signs of the world being awake just yet.

Thomas walks until finally, he reaches a small cave that looks over the sea. He nestles himself in as he watches the sunrise from the horizon. Thomas thanks the land for bringing him home.

He's grateful for having returned to Greece, but more importantly, perhaps he is blessed for having returned to himself. He thanks whatever higher-self within him helped him to take the unknown leap, but he would soon come to know that would change his life forever.

His flight takes off late that afternoon and he knows that he will one day return to this magical land and now he looks into the future, feeling ready to follow wherever it leads. Upon his return, Thomas spends a few months living with his parents in their country home.

Luckily his sister is happy to continue living in his apartment, offering him the time he needs to figure out what step to take next. In the meantime, he cooks, and cooks, and cooks until the refrigerator is empty of produce and stocked with savory plant-based meals.

He offers his mother two of her favorite traditional Greek foods he perfected. She is overjoyed by the delicious food he has prepared and by his rediscovered sense of purpose and inspiration.

Thomas enrolls in a culinary program upon returning home and soon after launches his own catering company. He focuses on bringing plants to plates in a way that feeds the souls of all nourishing both humans and the earth as one deeply integrated organism.

He starts off modestly, catering small events for his friends and family. Soon, however, his catering company blooms, touching the plates and palates of countless people across his country.

On the night after his first successful event, an event that brought city dwellers to the countryside for a feast beneath the stars, he dreams of another dream. This time, he rests on a beach on a faraway Greek island, looking out over the sea and thinking about how vast the ocean is he feels inspired and connected to both himself and to the world around him, sinking into the sand and listening to the waves rolled gently into and away from the shore.

It appears that nothing and everything happens in this dream, a feeling that has been with him since he first embarked on his Greek adventure many months ago. For the rest of his life, Thomas would often look back on his early days, thanking the unknown road for carrying him back to the roots. Each day he feels grateful for that first trip to Athens for it was that trip that changed everything.

Sleep Hypnosis for Deep Sleep and Relaxation (60mns)

Hello and welcome to this guided sleep hypnosis for deep sleep and relaxation. To begin, simply get into a comfortable position. It is recommended that you lie down in your bed and place your arms and legs however you want so long as it is comfortable for you. You will be here for quite a while and so comfort is of utmost importance. Without it, you will not be able to achieve deep relaxation.

At the end of this session, you will feel thoroughly relaxed and we can send you right off to sleep after this. So take a deep breath now to signal the body. To tell it that it is time to unwind, relax, and prepare for a night of restful sleep.

If you haven't already, go ahead and close your eyes. As your vision fades to black, shift your focus to your own breathing. Using your stomach, calmly breathe in and let the air flows in, filling your lungs entirely. Use your diaphragm to breathe, so that your lungs can be filled with air.

Focus on your breathing and use it to anchor yourself in the present moment. Just before you exhale, feel that gentle stillness in your body. Focus on how it feels. Observe every breath that you take and notice how relaxed your body becomes at each breath.

As you balance your awareness between the past and the future, there is a space. In this space between the past and the future is a freedom, a power, a silence, as you observe it, you notice its beauty.

It is calm. It is everything

If you observe your mind returning to the past or imagining the future, gently guide your focus back to the present. Be present in the present moment, allowing the observation of the breath to keep you present and centered. Allow yourself to relax at every exhale.

With the eyes closed, imagine standing on a beach on a beautiful spring day. To accommodate the gentle slope of the sand toward the water, you lean ever so slightly to the soothing and consistent tumble of the water's edge onto the shore as its timidly approaching and withdrawing as the small waves find their end.

Observe the tiny ripples over the surface of the water as the wind calmly travels on its way. You notice a subtle salty scent in the crisp fresh air, feeling happy and content. A gentle smile spreads on your face. This is a special place just for you this is your place.

Happy and content standing on the beach as you look out beyond the reef, you notice the distant hum at the same time as silent splashing of large waves colliding with the enormous rocks beyond the bay's calm water.

Looking back on the beach, you notice the resilient and lush plant life that leans onto the edge of the beach and toward the shore as best it can. Noticing the beautiful blue sky, you see a bird glide still as if floating on the breeze.

That same breeze gently cools the skin from the warmth of the sun. Scanning the surrounding further, you see that some leaves and foliage gently sway in the wind while others are perfectly still with surprising pockets of colorful wildflowers spread throughout the landscape.

At the end of the beach, you see the hues of grey and bronze on the surface of rocks. Rocks that have shared the beach with the wind, the water, and the sand for thousands of years, creating shapes beyond artistic imagination, creating an almost symbiotic relationship between nature's elements.

Feeling the sand underfoot, firm yet shaping to mold the base of the feet in this beautiful place, you feel so calm and relaxed. You see a beach chair sitting in the sand. Take yourself to that chair and rest comfortably.

In front of you now appears a large screen and, on that screen, you see all the things you do using energy to stay awake, every conceivable measure to prevent sleep see them all now on that screen.

Now if you sleep and rest thoroughly you will have an oversupply of energy. What would you really like to do with that energy? What constructive or instructive or developmental project would you like to undertake to use up that extra daily allotment of energy?

You've got to direct it elsewhere rather than keeping yourself awake. That nice rest each night is going to replenish your energy. how are you going to use it? As you contemplate this, you are projecting your thoughts onto the screen in front of you, allow these thoughts to roll like a movie reel as you watch on the screen all the things you would really like to do with that energy how are you going to use it

As those thoughts play on the screen in front of you, begin to elevate out of the body, leaving behind the thinking part of you in that beach chair to watch its thoughts without you as you drift away floating up, feeling free and liberated, distancing from your thoughts, feeling light and free as you float freely.

Within your mind, imagine a soft black velvet couch that has a warm and comfortable feel about it. It sits a large and wide. One end of the couch is shaped like a bed as you stretch out on the smooth soft velvet which feels ever so nice.

It creates within you a comfortable drowsy feeling. You take a deep relaxing breath as that feeling becomes more and more comforting, and all-encompassing as you drift off into the realms of sleep as thoughts into your mind allow these to drift across the soft black velvet and disappear off the edge then return to resting calmly and comfortably.

The sound of my voice just like a lullaby lets you sleep deeply and soundly feeling calm feeling safe and feeling relaxed. Distanced from your thoughts you rest and sleep easy knowing that all shall be well and now is the time for sleep.

Treating yourself to a night of deep and restful sleep. All shall be well. Each time you listen to this, you drift deeper and deeper into a calm and restful sleep easily and naturally sleeping deeply recovering and replenishing the mind and the body.

Sleep now, feeling relaxed and at peace. Sleep now calmly and deeply. All shall be well as thoughts into your mind allow the east to drift across the soft black velvet and disappear off the edge then return to resting calmly and comfortably in your mind as though these words are your own.

"As I sleep easily, I am filled with positive energy I sleep restfully and deeply as like leaves falling from a tree I let go of thoughts and worries allowing them to drop away. As I sleep freely and easily I am free from the past and the future all shall be well."

"I am filled with gratitude and peace as I sleep easily and peacefully, I am caring for myself and accepting the love within me. As I sleep deeply and restfully, I take care of my mind and body I sleep easily and at will, I sleep restfully and deeply. All shall be well."

Distanced from your thoughts you rest and sleep easy knowing that all shall be well and now is the time for sleep.

Treating yourself to a night of deep and restful sleep. All shall be well. Each time you listen to this, you drift deeper and deeper into a calm and restful sleep easily and naturally sleeping deeply recovering and replenishing the mind and the body.

Sleep now, feeling relaxed and at peace. Sleep now calmly and deeply. All shall be well as thoughts into your mind allow the east to drift across the soft black velvet and disappear off the edge then return to resting calmly and comfortably in your mind as though these words are your own.

"As I sleep easily, I am filled with positive energy I sleep restfully and deeply as like leaves falling from a tree I let go of thoughts and worries allowing them to drop away. As I sleep freely and easily I am free from the past and the future all shall be well."

"I am filled with gratitude and peace as I sleep easily and peacefully, I am caring for myself and accepting the love within me. As I sleep deeply and restfully, I take care of my mind and body I sleep easily and at will, I sleep restfully and deeply All shall be well."

Distanced from your thoughts you rest and sleep easy knowing that all shall be well and now is the time for sleep.

Treating yourself to a night of deep and restful sleep. All shall be well. Each time you listen to this, you drift deeper and deeper into a calm and restful sleep easily and naturally sleeping deeply recovering and replenishing the mind and the body.

Sleep now, feeling relaxed and at peace. Sleep now calmly and deeply. All shall be well as thoughts into your mind allow the east to drift across the soft black velvet and disappear off the edge then return to resting calmly and comfortably in your mind as though these words are your own.

"As I sleep easily, I am filled with positive energy I sleep restfully and deeply as like leaves falling from a tree I let go of thoughts and worries allowing them to drop away. As I sleep freely and easily, I am free from the past and the future all shall be well."

"I am filled with gratitude and peace as I sleep easily and peacefully, I am caring for myself and accepting the love within me. As I sleep deeply and restfully, I take care of my mind and body I sleep easily and at will, I sleep restfully and deeply All shall be well."

Each time you listen to this, you drift deeper and deeper into a calm and restful sleep easily and naturally, sleeping deeply recovering and replenishing the mind and the body sleep now feeling relaxed and at peace.

Sleep now.
Calmly and deeply. All shall be well.

As thoughts into your mind allow these to drift across the soft black velvet and disappear off the edge then return to resting calmly and comfortably in your mind as though these words are your own.

"As I sleep easily, I am filled with positive energy I sleep restfully and deeply as like leaves falling from a tree I let go of thoughts and worries allowing them to drop away. As I sleep freely and easily I am free from the past and the future all shall be well."

"I am filled with gratitude and peace as I sleep easily and peacefully, I am caring for myself and accepting the love within me. As I sleep deeply and restfully, I take care of my mind and body I sleep easily and at will, I sleep restfully and deeply. All shall be well."

Distanced from your thoughts, you rest and sleep easily, knowing that all shall be well, and now is the time for sleep, treating yourself to a night of deep and restful sleep. All shall be well.

Each time you listen to this, you drift deeper and deeper into a calm and restful sleep easily and naturally sleeping deeply recovering and replenishing the mind and the body sleep now feeling relaxed and at peace.

Sleep now.

Calmly and deeply. All shall be well.

As thoughts into your mind allow these to drift across the soft black velvet and disappear off the edge, then return to resting calmly and comfortably in your mind as though these words are your own.

"As I sleep easily, I am filled with positive energy I sleep restfully and deeply as like leaves falling from a tree I let go of thoughts and worries allowing them to drop away. As I sleep freely and easily, I am free from the past and the future all shall be well."

"I am filled with gratitude and peace as I sleep easily and peacefully, I am caring for myself and accepting the love within me. As I sleep deeply and restfully, I take care of my mind and body I sleep easily and at will, I sleep restfully and deeply. All shall be well."

Before Sleep Hypnosis for Relaxation (60mns)

Hello and welcome to this before sleep hypnosis for relaxation. In this session, we will be working toward relaxing the body and mind so that you can achieve a night of restful sleep. It is important that you have such a night of sleep as it provides you with the maximum energy and you will wake up the next day feeling fresh and ready to start the day.

So, without further ado, let's get started. Begin by getting into a comfortable position on your bed. It is recommended that you lie down and place your arms and legs however you like so long as you are comfortable. Comfort is of utmost importance, after all. If at any point during this session, you feel uncomfortable, you may move around gently to ease that discomfort.

Take a deep breath now to signal to the mind and body that it is time to unwind and relax. Allow yourself to bring your full awareness to your own complete comfort. If you haven't already, go ahead and close your eyes and shift your focus to your breathing as your vision fades to black.

This sleep hypnosis experience is all about letting go of your previous day. This trance experience will help you to let go of your past day's activities and any of your day's leftover thoughts and all of that day.

The time now spent energy just like soft echoes, disappearing in the distance as you comfortably and serenely falling into sleep. Now, imagine as best you can, effortlessly and completely releasing yourself from all of that daytime's physical stored tension as it also gives yourself the intention to release your mind's tensions.

Releasing from all of those weightier concerns by making a conscious choice to turn down all types of conscious thoughts and to turn down that more tiring, heavier, mental chatter.

They, just like you in these moments now, are choosing to move into all calming bedtime peace receiving the good news and the great news to further relax the conscious thinking mind.

And it's really a comforting and reassuring reason to pause all of those thoughts because there's really so very little here for the thinking mind to do, except to settle you back and to stretch you out more comfortably a little more and more.

Because even now, you're more comfortable, allowing yourself to let go and rest back, allowing yourself to become more in tune as your deeper ears continue to listen, allowing all of these powerful familiar sweeping automatic processes to proceed and unfold now as if all by themselves.

You know you're allowing your sleeping relaxation so swiftly and so speedily to slow all of those thoughts all the way down. You are resting your entire body now, feel every muscle lengthening and softening, becoming more and more relaxed as all parts of you, physically and mentally, increasingly relax, enjoying your whole, your body slowly unwinding and uncoiling, moving away from those old tensions.

And all of your own inner encouragement just remains as a peaceful reminder that you are in fact so safe and so in control of this session because you understand that really are all ready to descend even deeper and deeper into this blissful hypnosis.

Simply choosing to relax with all of those beautiful intentions to just easily sink you and relax you all of the ways down, as more and more parts of you are growing and unfolding you into your most powerful, peaceful, a blissful journey of sleep.

You're realizing you're moving so tranquil into those loveliest levels of the mind and your body feels entirely at peace. This arrival and this unfolding of your peace and your total relaxation only arrive as fast as you know. You can wish it as you choose to take in some slower and deeper and even more relaxing breaths.

These resting parts of you are realizing you're beginning to imagine in ways so much more because it's so pleasing for these parts of you - now just wander about as you wander and dream and let yourself dream of how deeply your deepest of all relaxations.

All of these relaxing sensations now progress inside of you even more, always unfolding you into calm within this space of your trancing mind. This full awareness allowing all of these calming resources to take you there.

It may be that very soon, there is some noticeable sense or feelings of even more serenity, moving you forward and yet simultaneously moving you deeper down, just moving you and traveling you in these relaxing beautiful ways as all of your trancing comforts becomes the relief of a day well spent.

And passing now as those echoes travel through you and into some unique and curious passages which will ease you through these states of peace and tranquility. It's the conscious mind back there that was holding so tightly onto all of that business and those more active thoughts.

As this freedom from conscious thought takes you more and more freely as you begin to float away, all of those ideas of wakefulness are really now dissolving so well and just evaporating.

At this moment, you know that everything is okay and that all will be well. It is very natural for all of those less conscious thoughts to also unfold as you move here and there and observe every passing thought like clouds drifting across the sky.

These thoughts also carry your awareness to wherever and whenever that may now be because so many more blissful and peaceful sensory inputs of that tranquility those calmest sensations really do begin to rock you so gently. Every passing second you spend here is another step further into relaxation.

And somehow these tingles of serenity and these vibrations of the bliss filling you so softly and gently with all new satisfactions and the joys of this deeper essence of pure asleep, arriving because your unconscious mind does remain aware of these words as it feels so safe to rest in these ways.

Focusing now so gently to be so easily open and receive all of these important messages of your growing calm. As you're aware of some even more subtle undercurrent and frequency of peace and serene transmissions just like restful delta waves of pure healing feeling inside of you with lasting elixir years of absolute peace.

Because all of these sounds and these words and these meanings you know are purely positive inspirations for your most restful self and all of these tunes are in ways are so frequently becoming so familiar and as welcoming to your total rest.

It was always encouraging you so gently to your total confidence, to really connect you, and help you and motivate you to get a real handle on those pillars and those foundations of relaxation.

As these very real foundations of your total calm are expanding and broadening your comforting self out every breath you take as you inhale slowly now is changing you with rejuvenation and every breath you braid out is transforming you with an even deeper bliss.

As this evolving yet simple process of your natural breathing continues all by itself, constantly releasing you from all tensions and all negativities and sometimes it's just as easy as that to imagine one by one or even all at once your subconscious enjoyment constantly delivering you with such a union of bliss into all of these natural ways into your most tranquil calm, as this deep flow is deeply unchaining you and unshackling you from everything unwanted.

All of those muscles are loosening and you feel all of those nerves and their fibers giving up their once held unwanted strains because relaxation now is quickly wrapping all around you and passing over and even into you just like a beautiful cloak of pure energy that melts away all the constrictions and opens your heart each and every time.

You now enjoy falling just like this into your absolute deepest of all deep sleep, because you're sleeping self is enjoying all of these entrancing kinds of states. You're always moving with your perfect natural resting pose and your own perfect tonics just like potions of inner health swirling and calming inside you.

As you move into your restful composure, these sensations pass down within you so easily and smoothly just like a soothing aromatic scent as your senses fill with that serenity. You can feel this relaxing aura flowing from the very top of your head, flowing down gently and ever so slowly, yet so soothing and relaxing and therapeutic, flowing just like honey, all the way down to the tip of your toes, covering you with a relaxing aura. You feel at ease, safe, relaxed, yet powerful, and confident at the same time.

And you're deliberately sending and receiving the sleeping health with such a beautiful and softly glowing beam of imagined white light just like a candle of constancy and blissful awareness, shining its protections all over you and penetrating each loosening muscle, throughout every lengthening joint, as these deeper words are reaching you.

You feel yourself growing softer and smoother inside like so many older leftover worries or concerns are disappearing, fading into thin air, leaving no trace behind, as if they are never there.

You are aware of your entire tangible essence, which is now receiving so much more beautiful relaxing aura into every cell because your inner core is now rejuvenating, and the essence of your vital being is beginning to quickly wind back because your inner glow of youthfulness and your vitality is now rebuilding and restoring and positively changing you inside in so many ways

As you reset your body's energetic clock and just like imagining those clocks hands moving backward, you're allowing all types of new and restorative health to repair you with these sensations in these visions with so much more health and healing restoring you and your youthful outlooks as you unlock this total rest.

So smoothly and efficiently. It's effortless. You feel yourself grow constantly here, and yet never a day older. You feel so much younger in this deeper mind as you gently enjoy rebalancing your inner happiness you are aware on some much, much deeper levels of your deepest self, so easily allowing you and opening you to release all of those special chemicals of sleep.

So many of those wonderfully felt natural endorphins of sleep are in pure health, because the more you do relax in this way and continue to enjoy all of these sounds and all of these healing healthy words, you feel you're sleeping more and more just like a baby sleep.

You feel that soothing caresses and sleeps frequencies and tones transform with pure repair, as the rest of that is already here, imagining so many subtle massaging softest waves bringing so many welcoming tingles of your flowing energy.

Your beautiful sleep continues to work, curate, and lengthen you as you continue to relax through all of this stretching moments because, in this slowing time of slumber, you're allowing all durations of your timely sleep to be so full and natural and extended to precisely the length of your very best duration of perfect rest.

As so many good feelings and wonderful feelings of satisfying, gratifying, sustained relief continue to carry you onwards and always deeper, with all of your days past energy now disappeared.

All of those days, past activities, you're saying, "So long, long gone". All of that old busyness is now completely spent as all of those long fading moments of those distant sunshine hours.

Now, all of these instead fade away into the mind as the mind rests. They fade into the distance just like the sunset on the horizon. You feel yourself gliding all the way down, slowly yet surely, deeper into relaxation, gently falling as a floating leaf.

Down, and down, down to meet your landing as you land into spacious peace. These lovely peaceful parts of you are landing and touching down so softly floating further onto a feathery pillow of absolute rest, or just like that floating ways as you see it move down to be gently carried away upon the loveliest the most caring bubbling types of crystal streams.

As all of these warming flowing waters unwind you inside and wash you, they relieve you of even more weight and you're breathing again with a sigh of deepest relief because you're unloading all of that worry, stress, or tension that may have been across your shoulders as you watch that floating leaf simply traveling and bobbing as it flows along those deepest rivers where you're observing all streams and their currents carrying away all leftover worry so far away.

As you continue to float so safely, you're moving out into that perfect source and arriving in this time to these soothing happiest dreams as you see yourself becoming so aligned and feel so light.

Here, we're coming just like light rays, becoming white, full of purity and perfection, transforming and changing you with such delight as twilight's deepest comforts continue to flow within you.

This peace always continues transforming you as you clear yourself and release more and more easily, removing any past concerns because you're releasing everything unwanted and just taking all of that away letting go of everything that is no longer required.

As you send those energies so far, far away and these inner sensations and these visions are now turning you because your most serene sensors are now beginning to ascend you, with the wings of your perfect calm sleeps, floating soaring and uplifting, or at least is now carrying your piece by piece. You're moving higher and higher within such parts of you becoming so free to fly out above.

And you're moving directly into all of your healthiest happiest enjoyable dreams now, throughout all of these infinite spaces of sleep's perfect ideals because you're ascending and becoming the very essence of this freedom, becoming just as those white rays now, moving you into that beyond all solar systems and or galaxies.

Your sleep is expanding beyond all of those heavens as you now see and imagine yourself just like a shining shooting star. You're moving with this clearest crystal light as if the lightness of the universe calls you to move even further beyond.

You're now moving into your sacred dream's space, feeling, and knowing that you will remain here because you're traveling through all the heavens. Your sleeping form is so sublime. You're so safe and protected here in your total rest and now allowing yourself to more deep sleep.

As all parts of your sleeping self are resetting you to your divine perfection, you're becoming once again just like one with this universe, so stunningly free and cleansed and released from all past energies.

Throughout all of your sleep, henceforth, you will rest more peacefully because you know that you will sleep so well after having experienced the magic if your deepest and best sleeping self.

You can sleep to your full and healthiest duration each and every time you choose to sleep and your bedtimes, you can easily and effortlessly fall fast asleep anytime you choose just as soon as your head touches that pillow or as soon as you decide to completely rest yourself down.

All of those thoughts and all aspects of your thinking mind are simply resting and all parts of your body are simply calming down. They know how to relax and they will send you into sleep immediately and instantaneously.

As you breathe deeply once again, and so calmly, so easily, imagine yourself lacing yourself into your total sleep because you are remaining here right now as you re-energized your deeper self and restoring your deeper self in all of these magical and positive ways as your inner being and your outer being remain so fast asleep, sleeping so well.

So, my lasting wish for you as your rest remains so pure is that you do easily and effortlessly sleep on and rest so deeply. Even as my voice and these words begin to fade, you know you continue to feel wonderfully good and positive each and every time you fall into your sleep.

Just as these moments right now, you're sleeping, and until we talk again, I wish you the very best. May you enjoy your most relaxing and pure sense of calm. May your restful sense of perfect continue as you sink deeper and deeper into sleep, and my voice becomes faint because you are resting and relaxing as you remain so deeply asleep.

Thank you and goodnight.

www.ingramcontent.com/pod-product-compliance
Lightning Source LLC
Chambersburg PA
CBHW070900080526
44589CB00013B/1139